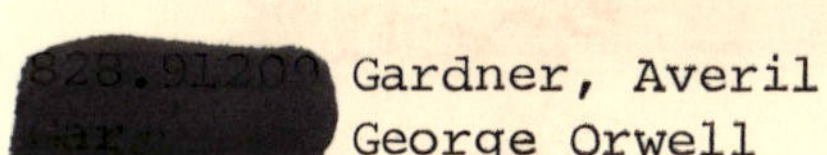

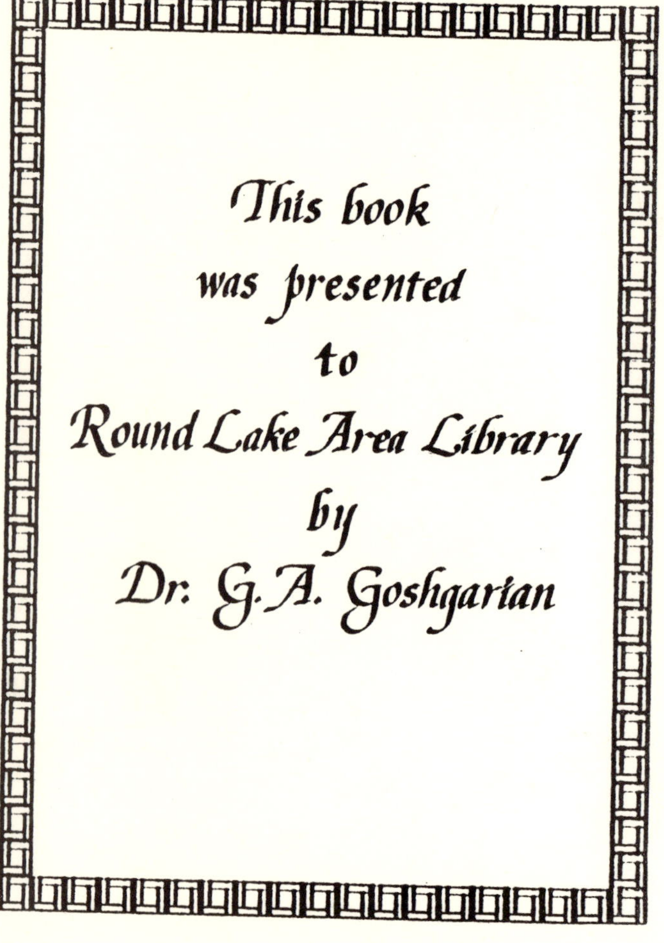
This book
was presented
to
Round Lake Area Library
by
Dr. G. A. Goshgarian

George Orwell

Twayne's English Authors Series

Kinley E. Roby, Editor

Northeastern University

TEAS 455

George Orwell

By Averil Gardner

Memorial University of Newfoundland

Twayne Publishers
A Division of G. K. Hall & Co. • Boston

George Orwell

Averil Gardner

Published by Twayne Publishers
A Division of G. K. Hall & Co.
70 Lincoln Street
Boston, Massachusetts 02111

Copyediting supervised by Lewis DeSimone
Book production by Janet Zietowski
Book design by Barbara Anderson

Typeset in 11 pt. Garamond
by Compset, Inc., of Beverly, Massachusetts

Printed on permanent/durable acid-free paper
and bound in the United States of America

Library of Congress Cataloging in Publication Data

Gardner, Averil.
George Orwell.

(Twayne's English authors series ; TEAS 455)
Bibliography: p.
Includes index.
1. Orwell, George, 1903–1950—Criticism and interpretation. I. Title. II. Series.
PR6029.R8Z637 1987 828′.91209 87-11908
ISBN 0-8057-6956-0

Contents

About the Author
Preface
Acknowledgments
Chronology

Chapter One
Eric Blair 1

Chapter Two
The Road to George Orwell 14

Chapter Three
An English Novelist in the 1930s 34

Chapter Four
Men and Brothers 63

Chapter Five
Orwell the Essayist 80

Chapter Six
Animal Farm 96

Chapter Seven
The Last Man in Europe: *Nineteen Eighty-Four* 108

Chapter Eight
"Farewell—and Hail" 124

Notes and References 135
Selected Bibliography 148
Index 154

About the Author

Averil Gardner was born in 1937 in London, England. After reading English Language and Literature at the University of London, she taught in Japanese universities, including Tsuda Women's University near Tokyo, from 1961 to 1964. She is currently Professor of English at Memorial University of Newfoundland, Canada. Her special areas of interest are medieval literature, Shakespeare, and the poetry and fiction of the nineteenth and twentieth centuries. She has published articles on medieval literature, Oscar Wilde, and Angus Wilson, in Japan, South Africa, the United States, and Canada. With Philip Gardner she is coauthor of *The God Approached: A Commentary on the Poems of William Empson* (Chatto & Windus, 1978). Her critical study of Angus Wilson, for Twayne's English Authors Series, was published in 1985.

Preface

Living and writing in the first half of the twentieth century, and dying at its exact midpoint, George Orwell might well, from beyond the grave, echo Tennyson's Ulysses to describe his reputation in the second half: "I am become a name." A large part of that name came to him in the last years of his life, with the publication of *Animal Farm* and *Nineteen Eighty-Four,* which reach with accidental symmetry equally backwards (to the Russian revolution of 1917) and forwards from the year 1950 when he died. Both books have become classics; the force of the latter was evidenced by the difficulty, in the actual year 1984, of registering that date as other than a phrase copyrighted by Orwell: his fiction had preempted history.

But if the year 1984 offered an all too convenient opportunity for concentrating a vivid searchlight on Orwell's last book, and for seeing him variously as sage, existential hero, and even political reactionary, it also rounded out three and a half decades during which most of Orwell's work, nonfiction as well as fiction, had been published or reissued, and subjected to intense and mostly favorable scrutiny. Thus, though Orwell has become a name—that of one of the most famous, and symptomatic, writers of the twentieth century—the name embraces more than the two novels that for so long were summoned up by it.

The years since Orwell's death have also been marked by an increasing wish to relate his work to his life, and to draw his life from the comparative obscurity in which, by forbidding a biography, Orwell had preferred in 1950 to leave it. Beginning in 1956 with a critical study by Christopher Hollis, Orwell's Eton contemporary, gathering detail through the researches of Peter Stansky and William Abrahams published in the 1970s, this quest for the Eric Blair who lay behind the pseudonym George Orwell culminated in 1980 in a monumental biography by Bernard Crick, to which writers on Orwell are likely to be indebted for many years.

This study is essentially concerned with Orwell's writings: his novels, his longer nonfiction, and (in chapter 5) his essays. These are dealt with in terms of their themes, their recurring motifs, and the varying success of their literary presentation. Since, however, Orwell's work grows naturally out of his response to the historical period in which he lived, and to the circumstances of his personal life, I have not confined biographical reference to his earliest, nonwriting years, but have interspersed my critical discussion throughout with those elements of individual and public history that seem to have a bearing on what, and how, Orwell wrote. The result, I hope, is a view of Orwell, as man and writer, that avoids the extremes of hagiography and belittlement alike, and represents him as a particular individual who in his best works succeeded in touching the common nerve of twentieth-century experience.

Averil Gardner

Memorial University of Newfoundland

Acknowledgments

I am grateful to the Memorial University of Newfoundland for a Vice-President's Special Research Grant, which enabled me to pursue research for this book at the George Orwell Archive, University College, London. I am also grateful for the generous help I received there from the archivist, Mrs. Janet Percival, and her staff.

Much assistance in my work was given to me by Lady Empson and Dr. George Rylands, who shared with me their memories of George Orwell at various stages of life; and by Miss Lettice Cooper, who kindly allowed me to see the last letter written to her by Eileen Blair. Mr. Francis King illuminatingly discussed with me Orwell's career and literary milieu. I am also glad to acknowledge help from two colleagues at Memorial University of Newfoundland, Mr. Tony Chadwick and Dr. John H. Evans. I am grateful to Mrs. Cathy Kieley for typing my manuscript, and particularly to my colleague and husband Philip Gardner for his most generous and patient help throughout.

I am grateful to A.M. Heath & Co., the Estate of the late Sonia Brownell Orwell, Secker & Warburg Ltd, and Harcourt Brace Jovanovich, Inc., for permission to quote from: *Down and Out in Paris and London, Burmese Days, A Clergyman's Daughter, Keep the Aspidistra Flying, Coming Up for Air, Homage to Catalonia* (copyright 1952, © 1980 by Sonia Brownell Orwell), *Animal Farm, Nineteen Eighty-Four, The Penguin Essays of George Orwell,* and *Collected Essays, Journalism and Letters of George Orwell* (© 1968 by Sonia Brownell Orwell).

Chronology

1903	Eric Arthur Blair born at Motihari, Bengal, India, 25 June, son of Richard Walmesley Blair and Ida Mabel Blair (née Limouzin).
1904	Brought to England by his mother. Family settles in Henley-on-Thames, Oxfordshire.
1908–1911	Educated at Sunnylands, an Anglican convent school in Henley.
1911–1916	Boarder at St. Cyprian's preparatory school, Eastbourne, Sussex.
1912	Richard Blair, retired from Indian Civil Service, returns to England. Family move to Shiplake near Henley.
1914	First work published, "Awake Young Men of England" (poem), in *Henley and South Oxfordshire Standard.*
1915	Blair family moves back to Henley.
1917	Spends Lent term at Wellington College.
1917–1921	King's Scholar, Eton College.
1921	Parents move to Southwold, Suffolk, December.
1922	Blair attends cramming establishment in Southwold, January to June, to prepare for India Office examinations.
1922–1927	Assistant Superintendent of Police, Indian Imperial Police, Burma.
1928–1929	Lives in Paris, writing and later working as a dishwasher. In Hôpital Cochin, Paris, with pneumonia, February 1929.
1930–1931	Goes tramping and hop-picking in London and Home Counties area. Writes early version ("A Scullion's Diary") of *Down and Out in Paris and London.* Begins to contribute reviews to *Adelphi.* Earliest essays ("The Spike" and "A Hanging") published in *Adelphi,* April and August 1931, under his own name.

1932–1933 Teaches at the Hawthorns, a small private school in Hayes, Middlesex.

1933 First book, *Down and Out in Paris and London,* published by Victor Gollancz, January. Pseudonym "George Orwell" used for this book and retained for future books. Teaches at Frays College, Uxbridge, Middlesex, September to December. Hospitalized with pneumonia, December.

1934 Gives up teaching. Spends ten months in Southwold. *Burmese Days* published in United States, October. Moves to Hampstead, London, November.

1934–1935 Works as part-time assistant in Booklovers' Corner, a bookshop in Hampstead. *A Clergyman's Daughter* published, March 1935. *Burmese Days* published in England, June 1935. Meets Eileen O'Shaughnessy, aged thirty.

1936 In industrial Lancashire and Yorkshire, investigating working-class life and unemployment at suggestion of Victor Gollancz, January to March. Moves to Wallington, Hertfordshire, April. *Keep the Aspidistra Flying* published, June. Marries Eileen O'Shaughnessy. Attends Independent Labour Party Summer School, Letchworth, Hertfordshire, July. Leaves for Spain, December.

1937 In Spain, January to June. Corporal (later lieutenant) with P.O.U.M. detachment on the Aragon front. Involved in street fighting in Barcelona between government and Anarchist troops. Wounded in throat by sniper near Huesca. Honorably discharged for medical reasons from P.O.U.M. militia. Evades arrest during anti-P.O.U.M. purge in Barcelona. *The Road to Wigan Pier* published, March. Left Book Club edition of more than forty thousand copies.

1938 In tuberculosis sanatorium, Aylesford, Kent, March to August. *Homage to Catalonia* published, April. Joins Independent Labour Party, June. Goes to Morocco for health reasons, September.

1939 Returns to England, March. *Coming Up for Air* published, June. Death of father.

1940	*Inside the Whale* published, March. Moves from Wallington back to London, May. (Resides at various addresses in London until 1946.) Reviewing for *Time and Tide* and *Tribune.* Joins Local Defence Volunteers (Home Guard), June. Made a sergeant.
1941	*The Lion and the Unicorn* published, February.
1941–1943	Talks Producer, Empire Department, British Broadcasting Corporation, in charge of broadcasting to India and Southeast Asia. Death of mother, March 1943.
1943–1946	Literary Editor of *Tribune.*
1944	Orwell and Eileen adopt a one-month-old baby, whom they name Richard Horatio Blair.
1945	War correspondent for the *Observer* in Paris and Cologne, March to May. Death of wife while under anaesthetic for an operation, 29 March. Covers first postwar election campaign, June to July. *Animal Farm* published, August.
1946	*Critical Essays* published, February. Moves to Barnhill, Isle of Jura, May.
1947	Enters Hairmyres Hospital, near Glasgow, with tuberculosis of the left lung, Christmas Eve.
1948	Returns from hospital to Jura, July. Completes revision of *Nineteen Eighty-Four* by December.
1949	Enters the Cotswold Sanatorium, Cranham, Gloucestershire, January. *Nineteen Eighty-Four* published, June. Over four hundred thousand copies sold within one year. Transferred from Cranham to University College Hospital, London, September. Marries Sonia Brownell, an editorial assistant with *Horizon,* in hospital, 13 October.
1950	Dies suddenly in University College Hospital, of a hemorrhaged lung, 21 January. Buried in the churchyard of All Saints, Sutton Courtenay, Berkshire.

Chapter One
Eric Blair

The time was August 1914, just after the outbreak of World War I. The place was the village of Shiplake, on the Oxfordshire side of the river Thames, between Reading and Henley. Three children, playing in a garden at the end of the summer holidays, looked across the fence and saw a boy of about their own age who was standing on his head. With the ordinary directness of children, they asked him why. He answered equally directly, but with a detachment and a perspicuity far from ordinary for a boy of eleven. He was doing it because "you are noticed more if you stand on your head than if you are the right way up."[1]

The boy was Eric Blair. His action had certainly gained the attention of the three children, whose name was Buddicom, and led immediately to a lasting friendship. His explanation of that action had a prophetic accuracy and can almost serve as the emblem of his career. In 1933 he drew the attention of his early readers with his book *Down and Out in Paris and London,* a look at society from underneath, and the pen name he used for that and all subsequent books, George Orwell, came to stand for an approach to life that was always unexpected and that has, particularly since his death in 1950, compelled generations of readers to reassess and expand their own opinions and angles of view. And just as the adoption of a pen name can itself be considered as a sort of standing on one's head, (both for disguise of self and for the discovery of hidden truth), so Orwell's last book, his novel *Nineteen Eighty-Four,* took the realities of the year in which he wrote it, 1948, and projected them—inside out or upside down—into a vision of the future that for many remains full of foreboding, even if not precisely realized in the actual year 1984.

Early Childhood and Education

Eric Arthur Blair was born on 25 June 1903 in Motihari, an Indian town some twenty-five miles south of the Nepalese border, in the then

British province of Bengal but now in the state of Bihar. He was the second child, and only son, of Richard Walmesley Blair, a forty-six-year-old official—a peripatetic and never very exalted one—of the Opium Department of the government of India. In *The Road to Wigan Pier* (1937), George Orwell described his earlier but never completely abandoned self as having been born into the "lower-upper-middle class," that is, toward the bottom end of a salary spectrum running from two to three thousand pounds a year.[2] By that time, more than thirty years on, Orwell had become a socialist concerned with describing the condition of the working classes in the north of England, and it seems likely that he wished the word "lower" to carry an overtone that might identify him with those he was writing about. Nevertheless, it would not do to forget the "upper-middle" it modifies: the decisiveness and opinionatedness of so much of George Orwell's writing, whatever its end, takes its origin from the social position of Eric Blair, whose father, however humbly placed in it, was a member of the ruling class.

Richard Blair's own father, Thomas Blair (1802–1867), was educated at Pembroke College, Cambridge (though only for a year), was ordained in Calcutta in the Anglican church, served many years in "the colonies" and ended up as a vicar in rural Dorset; his father, Charles Blair (1743–1820), owned plantations in Jamaica and married Lady Mary Fane, daughter of the Earl of Westmorland, though his considerable fortune had dwindled by the time Thomas, his tenth son, was born. Eric Blair could trace his descent back to aristocracy and former affluence, and his evolution into the writer George Orwell, who glimpsed the renewal of affluence in the very last years of his life, proceeded for its first twenty-five years along lines that, despite his parents' modest income, were laid down by his upper-middle-class, imperialist heritage.

Eric Blair's mother, born Ida Mabel Limouzin, was more lively and less conventional than her husband, and eighteen years younger. Her French father was a teak merchant and boat-builder in Moulmein in southern Burma; her English mother was still living there when Blair went out to Burma nineteen years later. Meanwhile, like most sons of colonial administrators, Eric Blair had experienced a boarding-school education "back home." In 1904, he and his mother (together with his elder sister, Marjorie, then six) went to England, living first in Henley-on-Thames, where from 1908 to 1911 he attended a small school, Sunnylands, operated by a Anglican convent. He saw little of his father until the latter retired to England in 1912; his home life, spent largely among women, appears to have been a happy one, though he experienced chest trouble, in the form of bronchitis, as early as his second year, and because of the five-year age gap between himself and his elder sister felt a certain degree of isolation. But there were frequent expeditions into the Thames valley country around Henley, and at an early age he was introduced to the pleasures of fishing. Both these aspects of his childhood were fictionalized later into a prewar golden age, particularly in his novel *Coming Up for Air* (1939).

Eric Blair did sufficiently well at Sunnylands to be recommended for entrance to St. Cyprian's, an expensive preparatory school founded in 1899 and situated in Eastbourne, a superior seaside resort on the Sussex coast. St. Cyprian's, run by an ambitious couple, the Vaughan Wilkeses, had had in its short existence remarkable success in coaching its pupils for scholarships to the most prestigious English public schools, especially Harrow and Eton. Since Blair seemed a potential winner of such a scholarship, likely to increase the school's academic and social prestige and thus its profitability to its owners, he was accepted at half-fees, to begin in September 1911. His father retired from the Indian Civil Service in 1912 on a pension of £438 a year—a not inconsiderable sum, but St. Cyprian's full-fee tuition would have cost over a third of it—too much to spend on the education of only one of three children.[3] Thus it came about that Blair entered the company of boys whose families were, in the main, far richer than his own, a situation that as the author of *Keep the Aspidistra Flying* (1936) he was to deplore.[4]

In terms of the academic results they eventually produced, Blair's five years at St. Cyprian's were well spent: he won two scholarships, one to Wellington, the public school particularly associated with the army;[5] and another, of far greater academic distinction and financial value, to Eton, the most famous public school in Britain. That the forcing-house educational methods of St. Cyprian's had much to do with Blair's success is shown by contrasting them to his Eton experience, where a far more liberal atmosphere left him free not to do "a stroke of avoidable work."[6] As this reaction suggests, he felt no gratitude to St. Cyprian's for pushing him on, or for taking him at half-fees, a fact that, though properly concealed from the other boys and at first from himself, was later thrown in his face by the unimaginative headmaster and his emotionally overbearing wife in order to pressure him into working harder. For these two (derisively nicknamed "Sambo" and "Flip"), and for the school ethos, built on rote learning, favoritism, and snobbery, Blair harbored a detestation he never overcame; it finally surfaced in the 1940s in his long essay "Such, Such Were the Joys," perhaps the most withering attack ever written about the English preparatory school.[7]

Cyril Connolly, Blair's contemporary at St. Cyprian's, and, later, editor of the magazine *Horizon,* had already written about the school much more briefly in his book *Enemies of Promise.*[8] His general picture of the school and its proprietors confirms Blair's, so that one cannot accuse the latter's essay of being a fabrication, whether or not its famous description of Blair's being beaten for wetting his bed is literally true in all details.[9] But Connolly's comparative lack of emphasis—he mentions only in passing the "fetid plunge-bath"[10] that occupies so many lines in Orwell's essay, and accepts as a fact of life the bullying and the variation of pupils in "favour" with Mrs. Wilkes, which bothered Blair to an extreme degree—leaves one with the feeling that Blair took deeply to heart matters that for others were part of the unavoidable process of education. One may say either that Connolly was tougher and more "balanced" than Blair, or that Blair's rebelliousness and resentment were the functions of an intelligence marked already by factual clear-sightedness and disenchantment, in contrast with the romantic aestheticism of Connolly. But however one assesses "Such, Such Were the Joys" as evidence for an indictment, either of St. Cyprian's or of Blair, what is apparent is that the school planted in Blair, or perhaps increased in him,[11] a sense of personal failure, of being alienated from a privileged society to whose rules and taboos he was unable to conform.[12]

Nothing of this, however, is visible in the various letters he wrote from St. Cyprian's to his mother between 1911 and 1914. These, exceedingly ill-spelled at first, are concerned with thanks for presents received, inquiries after family pets—a cat, a guinea pig, white mice, tadpoles—and academic and sporting activities. On Sunday, 11 October 1911, he wrote: "I am top in arithmetic," and in football "I shot seven goals." On one occasion he describes a fancy dress dance he attended as "a footman with a red velvet coat . . . a lace frill and a wig."[13] The letters entail no more than the small change of schoolboy correspondence, perhaps implying loneliness in requests for news of home, and sometimes brightened by mentions of such items as a "wreck a good way out" in the English Channel, a day off spent rambling on the South Downs behind Eastbourne, and, in the only passage that hints at the Orwellian style to come, a description of Blair's nervous prowess as a goalkeeper: "most of the chaps the other side were awful rats and they were running at me like angry dogs."[14]

Whatever his objections to the St. Cyprian's ethos of money, "character," and success, Blair was no pale "sensitive" who quailed at sport. Nor was he impervious to the upsurge of popular emotion that accompanied the outbreak of the Great War in August 1914. His earliest publications were two short patriotic poems, derivative but creditable for his age, which appeared in October 1914 and July 1916 in his local paper, the *Henley and South Oxfordshire Standard,* and were read at school. The first, "Awake Young Men of England," was a boisterous call to enlistment; the second, on a subject set by Mrs. Wilkes herself for a school poetry competition, was a sober elegy for Lord Kitchener, drowned when his ship was sunk en route to Russia. In view of Blair's lifelong devotion to his country, and to the best in "Englishness," there is no reason to suspect the sincerity of his sentiments at this time. Only a month before "Kitchener" was published, Blair had won his scholarship to Eton. It is hard to believe that these two successes did not bring him some genuine "favour" at school, and even sweeten for a while his own feelings about it. But he admitted nothing of the kind in "Such, Such Were the Joys," and once he left St. Cyprian's in December 1916, he never returned there, unlike Cyril Connolly, who followed close on his heels to Eton.

Eton College usually accepted not more than fourteen King's Scholars each year. Blair had ranked fourteenth in the 1916 election,[15] an exceptionally brilliant one, and a vacancy was not immediately available for him. As a temporary measure he took up his other scholarship, to Wellington, and spent the first nine weeks of 1917 in its uncongenial, militaristic atmosphere. When a place came up at Eton he was glad to take it, entering in May 1917, just a month before his fourteenth birthday.

Bernard Crick, Orwell's most exhaustive biographer, has aptly characterized the milieu in which Blair now found himself as "an intellectual elite, thrust into the heart of a social elite."[16] The social elite consisted of nine hundred "Oppidans" living in various houses scattered around the small town of Eton; Blair was one of only seventy "Collegers," the academic cream of the school who lived in the oldest buildings, wore gowns on top of their Eton suits, and paid fees of only twenty-five pounds a year in contrast to the one hundred pounds paid by Oppidans. Blair called his fees "exorbitant," but one takes this as an attention-seeking device, a piece of youthful bloody-mindedness, not as a considered statement.[17]

By contrast with St. Cyprian's, Eton was not only cheaper, but offered a liberal academic climate and far less bullying, especially in college. In addition, though the corporal punishment of younger boys by senior boys was normal at Eton as at other public schools, the 1916 election to which Blair belonged had a decided aversion to imposing its seniority by force and largely discontinued the practice when it reached the top of the school: in *Enemies of Promise* Connolly referred to it as an "oasis of enlightenment."[18] After the Second World War, when the British educational system was in process of alteration under the influence of the Labour government, Orwell wrote in the *Observer* that he saw little likelihood of Eton's surviving "in anything like its present form," but he nevertheless acknowledged its "one great virtue," that it was "a tolerant and civilized atmosphere which gives each boy a fair chance of developing his individuality."[19]

Blair's own response to Eton's tolerant atmosphere took the form of not exerting himself at academic work. In 1917 he was low in his class lists for all his subjects, Latin, Greek, French, mathematics, science, and divinity. A change from the arts to the science side, mainly biology, made no difference, so he soon switched back, and by the end of 1918 he was taking only "General Division" subjects, that is, "a general education for non-university streams."[20] He did best at French, for which his teacher was for a short time Aldous Huxley, whose distinctive style of speech fascinated him; but on a form list of 149 boys his position was no better than 117th, and by the time of his final Eton examinations, in July 1921, he ranked only 138th out of 167. Recognizing quite early Blair's reluctance to push himself (and deploring it), his tutor A. S. F. Gow, a distinguished classical scholar and fellow of Trinity College, Cambridge, encouraged him to compose "not the weekly essays exacted by most tutors, but fables, short stories, accounts of things liked and disliked"[21]—a regime whose effect prefigured his writing career as George Orwell.

Undistinguished as was his academic career at Eton ("always a bit of a slacker and a dodger" was how Gow in old age described him),[22] Blair was by no means unnoticed by his schoolmates. His contemporary Roger Mynors, later professor of Latin at Oxford, remembered him as a constant arguer; Steven Runciman, later the author of *History of the Crusades,* became quickly aware that he "had read a lot of very unusual books"[23]—the complete published works, in fact, of John Galsworthy, H. G. Wells and George Bernard Shaw, as well as Samuel Butler's *The Way of All Flesh.* He was known, according to Cyril Connolly, as "the Election atheist,"[24] though this did not prevent him from being confirmed into the Church of England, by the Bishop of Oxford, in November 1918, and from leaving instructions in his will that he wished to be buried according to Anglican rites. Christopher Hollis, later a Conservative Member of Parliament, recalled Blair's hatred for the normal courtesy of touching one's cap when passing a monitor; in this he was unusual, but far less so when he participated in making fun of the jingoistic peace celebrations organized by the Eton O.T.C. (Officer Training Corps) and held in the school yard in 1919.[25] This was no more than the standard antiwar sentiment at that time; less acceptable was his habit, after family visits to the school, of belittling his own parents to his school friends, and of ridiculing the appearance of other boys' parents.[26] "I don't think he was very kind," recalled Runciman, who was a good friend of Blair at Eton.[27]

Putting things broadly, and using a distinction between human types common at this time, one may say that Blair was more of a "hearty" than an "arty" while at Eton; though he was less either of these than one who stood apart. George Rylands, himself an aesthete and later to win distinction as a fellow of King's College, Cambridge, and a shaper of Shakespearean theatrical tradition, has described Blair, one year his junior at Eton, as "impassive and aloof."[28] In 1920 Rylands produced a splendid *Twelfth Night,* himself memorably playing the part of Viola; Blair first "derided the venture" but later agreed to be a nonspeaking "officer."[29] In 1921 he played a shepherd in the Eton production of *The Winter's Tale.* In the field of journalism he helped to edit and produce the *Election Times,* a handwritten periodical that cost one penny to read and sixpence to buy, which no one ever did; and a number of issues of *College Days,* to which he contributed poems of no particular merit. But Blair seems to have been at least as occupied with physical pleasures: he may have ridiculed the peace celebrations of the O.T.C., but he enjoyed its annual camp, and was a good shot with a service rifle. He liked fives, and taking part in scratch games of cricket; he loved swimming; more unconventionally for an Etonian, he also fished for pike in "Jordan," a small tributary of the Thames. All these were also the pleasures of his vacations, often spent with the Buddicom children whom he had first met in the summer of 1914.

At the end of his time at Eton, October 1921, he achieved perhaps his greatest schoolboy distinction, when by means of an adroit pass he made it possible for his friend Robert Longden to score a goal in the Eton wall game, that arcane and very rough college sport in which a goal was almost unheard of. His final academic results at Eton were dismal, however, which ruled out the likelihood of his winning a scholarship to Oxford—even assuming he had wished to go there, which seems doubtful. The pattern of life out of which his books were in part to spring was forecast not by any devotion to the academic life of Eton but rather by two revealing incidents. One, recalled later by Christopher Hollis, was Blair's offering of himself as a solitary scapegoat on behalf of his classmates, when an offended sixth-former was about to beat them all for impudence: the gesture was unavailing.[30] The other was described by himself in a contemporary letter to Runciman as his "first adventure as an amateur tramp." On his way, in August 1920, to spend part of his summer vacation in Cornwall, he missed his train connection at Plymouth; not having enough money for both food and bed, he chose the former, and spent a very cold night in the corner of a field with only his cape around him. Arriving finally at Looe by an early morning train, "I was forced to walk four miles in the hot sun; I am very proud of the adventure but would not repeat it."[31] The incident was vividly described, and Blair's temporary "outsider" stance was frequently to be repeated, and sought, in adult life.

Schools of Experience

During the latter years of the war Blair's parents were away from their house in Henley-on-Thames, both of them "doing their bit" for the war effort. Though sixty, Richard Blair joined the army, becoming reputedly its oldest second lieutenant and taking charge of a mule depot in Marseilles; Ida Blair, at forty-two, worked as a clerk in the Ministry of Pensions in London and lived in a very small apartment in Earl's Court. Many of Eric's vacations, during and after the war, were spent with the Buddicom family, sometimes at Henley, sometimes near Church Stretton in Shropshire, and finally, in the summer of 1921, at Rickmansworth just northwest of London, where the Blairs, who had decided to move from Henley, had temporarily rented a house, which they shared with the Buddicoms. These holidays satisfied two sides of Blair's nature. One was active and unreflective: with Prosper Buddicom, a Harrow schoolboy one year his junior, he went fishing, did a lot of shooting (of birds and rabbits, not at targets), burned gunpowder on a bonfire, and attempted to make nitroglycerin and bombs. On one occasion they assembled an amateur whiskey still, which blew up. Blair's more sensitive and literary side came out in his friendship with Prosper's sister Jacintha, two years older than himself. To her he often spoke of his intention to become a "famous author,"[32] though he was quite happy to envisage himself in this role as E. A. Blair. Eric, he felt, was not an author's name. The two of them exchanged and discussed books: detective stories, ghost stories, including Henry James's *The Turn of the Screw,* H. G. Wells's long story "The Country of the Blind," and the work of Dickens and Shakespeare. Blair was "continually concocting long historical dramas in blank verse, which he read aloud to me with different voices for different parts."[33]

Jacintha Buddicom appears to have been Blair's first serious romantic attachment, though an Eton letter from him to Cyril Connolly confessed a crush on another boy, a normal enough occurrence in a single-sex school.[34] Jacintha's feelings, though very friendly, were not particularly romantic. Blair's description of Jacintha and himself, in a poem of autumn 1918 entitled "The Pagan," as "Naked souls alive and free," prompted the prim response that for "naked" he should have written "unarmoured." Clearly the poem's conclusion, "That mystic light is in your eyes / And ever in your heart will shine," was inappropriate to one so realistic and sensible. By the summer of 1921 Blair was expressing naked disappointment: "My love can't reach your heedless heart at all." Jacintha's reply, advising him not to be dazzled "By light / Too Bright" but rather to "rest / In tranquil shade," shows that he had reason to do so.[35] Blair recalled their friendship, and his disappointment, in 1949, when he wrote to Jacintha Buddicom after a separation of nearly twenty-eight years: "You were such a tender-hearted girl, always full of pity for the creatures we others shot and killed. But you were not so tender-hearted to me when you abandoned me to Burma with all hope denied."[36]

It seems unlikely, however, that Blair's decision to go to Burma, as distinct from anywhere else, had anything to do with "rejection" by Jacintha. More simply, it was a question of what he should do on leaving Eton, which he did in December 1921. In that same month his parents had moved to Southwold, on the Suffolk coast between Lowestoft and Aldeburgh; it was a quiet resort town, then becoming popular as a haven for retired Anglo-Indian officials. Blair joined them there, and spent six months at a local cramming establishment, preparing himself for the entrance examinations set by the India Office:

not in order to qualify for the Indian Civil Service, whose prerequisite was the university degree rendered inaccessible by Blair's poor performance at Eton, but for the Indian Imperial Police, whose standard was less exacting than that required for university entrance.

Jacintha Buddicom, writing many years later, attributed Blair's joining the Indian police to his father's "adamant" pressure on him to follow in the "parental footsteps."[37] Fatherly suggestion, rather than insistence, may have been all that was necessary; Etonians in the British colonial police were admittedly rare,[38] but Blair's school performance had reduced his options, and such a post would seem a good deal more glamorous than that of schoolmaster or office clerk. Given Ida Blair's earlier life in Burma, her son's first choice of that country on his list of preferences submitted to the India Office need not seem at all surprising; members of her family were still there, and she may have implanted in her son, who grew up largely apart from his father until the age of nine, a romantic notion of the exotic and mysterious East. Steven Runciman was quite definite about Blair's positive wish, expressed at Eton, to go to Burma: "He had hardly known it, but he always used to talk about it. That was where he wanted to go back to . . . it was at the back of his mind . . . I think all through his school days."[39] And if Blair had really been belatedly sorry to have missed the chance of Oxford, the fulfillment of such a longer-standing dream, with its possibilities of an exciting outdoor life, might well have seemed a satisfactory substitute.

Having passed his examinations, Blair sailed for Burma in October 1922, a few months after his nineteenth birthday. As one of a number of new English recruits, he underwent a nine-month period of training at the Burma Provincial Police Training School in Mandalay, followed by a further fifteen months of probationary field assignments, which varied between headquarters administrative and clerical work and tours of inspection in the villages. Blair's rank during this period, largely spent in the humid flatlands of the Irrawaddy Delta near Rangoon, was Probationary Assistant Superintendent of Police, a position whose mixture of actual junior status and highsounding nomenclature captures that instant dignity and upward mobility conferred on British officials serving in an imperial capacity. Training was in police methods and in languages, Burmese and Hindustani, that Blair seems to have experienced little difficulty in learning—even to the extent, a police contemporary reported, of being able to converse in Burmese with Buddhist priests.[40]

The friendliness of rulers and ruled suggested by this was not, however, characteristic of Anglo-Burmese relations at this time. Burma, administered as a province of the Indian Empire, had been initially excluded from the reforms that in 1919 brought a token measure of representation for Indians in elected assemblies and in the senior ranks of the Indian Civil Service. These reforms were extended to Burma in 1923, but by then the resentment caused by their denial had soured relations irreversibly, so that the period during which Blair was in Burma, from November 1922 until the summer of 1927, was a tense and difficult one. Maung Htin Aung, later Vice-Chancellor of the University of Rangoon but then a freshman there, wrote in 1971 of the hostility to British rule expressed by Burmese university students and Buddhist priests, and gave an eyewitness account of an incident in 1924 in which Blair was involved. Pushed, probably accidentally, by a student down the stairs of a railway station in suburban Rangoon, Blair furiously "raised the heavy cane that he was carrying, to hit the boy on the head, but checked himself and struck him on the back instead."[41] Much altercation ensued, but luckily matters did not escalate beyond that. One may feel that Blair's reaction was unduly irritated, or that, given his official position, he showed considerable self-restraint. Either way, it is not difficult to imagine, even without the different sort of evidence provided by his essays "A Hanging" (1930) and "Shooting an Elephant" (1936), how Blair must gradually have come to feel, in the words of Gilbert and Sullivan's *The Pirates of Penzance,* that, in Burma, a policeman's lot was not a happy one.

Unlike the letters he wrote to his mother from St. Cyprian's, Blair's letters home from Burma have not survived. It is hard to imagine that he did not write any, if only to describe something of his life as an official to his civil service father, or to give Ida Blair news of her mother, still living in Moulmein when he was posted there for an eight-month tour of duty in April 1926. The Limouzins were comfortably well off and did a lot of entertaining; Mrs. Limouzin, who liked to wear Burmese dress but could not speak the language, was "a leading figure in the British community."[42] Also in Moulmein was an aunt of Blair's, married to a senior official in the forestry service. Thus Blair had no need to feel utterly isolated in a strange land. He did, in fact, have some enjoyments in Burma, shooting pigeons, buying himself a large American motorcycle, and being able to get into Rangoon fairly frequently when stationed nearby in an otherwise uncongenial post at Syriam, where he helped to guard the Burmese Oil Company's refinery. Nevertheless, in a number of descriptions of him furnished by people who met him in Burma, the recurrent word is "shy," and whereas his colleagues in the police spent their evenings drinking in the mess or in British-only clubs, Blair seems to have kept more to himself and read a great deal. Jacintha Buddicom, who received three letters from him, recalled many years later that the first was "in the strain 'You could never understand how awful it is if you hadn't been here'—very disconsolate, but unspecific."[43]

Blair's essay "A Hanging," published in the *Adelphi* under his own name in 1931, makes plain one of the simplest reasons for his distress: his identification with a judicial system that took human life. Like Oscar Wilde, with whose poem *The Ballad of Reading Gaol* (1898) Blair's essay has something in common, he could not come to terms with the physical reality of capital punishment, "the unspeakable wrongness of cutting a life short when it is in full tide."[44] In *The Road to Wigan Pier,* where he spoke at some length of his gradually increasing hatred for "the imperialism I was serving," he stated that "it needs very insensitive people to administer . . . our criminal law" (246). Whether or not such a statement is a slur on policemen, it is apparent that Blair was not equipped to be one, whatever ambitions he might have harbored when he went to Burma. Nor, as indicated by "Shooting an Elephant"—the description of an incident that took place during his tour in Moulmein—could he easily sustain the mask of the "sahib," which required him to impress the "natives" by apparently taking charge of events while really being controlled by them. For Blair, his shooting of the elephant, an only equivocally necessary act, was done "solely to avoid looking a fool" in the eyes of the large Burmese crowd that had followed him.[45] It is an open question whether Blair's presentation of the incident does not reveal his own limitations as well as the paradox of imperialism he used it to illustrate: "I perceived in this moment that when the white man turns tyrant it is his own freedom that he destroys."[46] It is possible that a cooler-headed, or more arrogant, official would have ignored the crowd's silent collective will and left the now calmer elephant alone. Clearly Blair was no such person, being conscious both of the falseness of the whole imperialistic position, what in 1929 he described as "despotism . . . hidden . . . in a mask of democracy,"[47] and of the hatred that, as a policeman, he himself excited. Perhaps the fairest comment to make is that his experience in Burma simultaneously aroused Blair's political and humanitarian consciousness and demonstrated to him his personal unsuitability for his official role.

Blair's last assignment came in December 1926, to Katha in Upper Burma, halfway between Mandalay and Myitkina. Ironically, it was the most congenial landscape he had worked in, "luxuriant jungle, open hills and river meadows, exotic with flowers and vegetation, and a dry, not too hot, atmosphere";[48] the degree to which he responded to its attractiveness can be judged from the lyrical descriptions in his first novel, *Burmese Days* (1934). Nevertheless, entitled to home leave in November 1927, after five years in the police service, he applied for it on unspecified medical grounds after only six months at Katha. He was granted a period of five months' leave to commence in July 1927, and returned to England, by ship as far as Marseilles, then via Paris, where he visited his aunt Nellie, another Limouzin relative. In his essay "Why I Write" (1946), he stated that "from a very early age . . . I knew when I grew up I should be a writer. Between the ages of seventeen and twenty-four I tried to abandon this idea."[49] Perhaps the second sentence is not completely true: in Burma he wrote at least three poems, read a great deal, and must, if only by comparison with his fellow policemen and colonial officials, have realized that the "arty" side of his nature was deeper-seated than he had thought when he embarked for Burma. Arriving back in England at a little over twenty-four, he made his break with an uncongenial career final: he submitted his resignation from the Indian Imperial Police, and set his course toward becoming a writer.

Chapter Two
The Road to George Orwell

His experience in Burma gave Blair the groundwork for his first novel, *Burmese Days,* though he did not begin serious work on it until late in 1930, and the book was not published until 1934. He did, however, as early as 1927 and 1928,[1] draft some pages dealing with that novel's main character, John Flory, whom he presented as dying in 1927 (the year of his own return from Burma), and as composing for himself a sardonic "epitaph." Its middle stanza runs thus:

> He has spent sweat enough to swim in
> Making love to stupid women;
> He has known misery past thinking
> In the dismal art of drinking.

The distinct ring in this of the poetry of A. E. Housman may have been prompted by a meeting with Housman at a dinner soon after Blair's return to England. Housman questioned him about Burma.

It would be helpful to know what Blair replied. Instead, one must rely, though with some care, on the hindsight remarks he made, as Orwell, for the benefit of the general reader in *The Road to Wigan Pier,* the mixture of documentary, autobiography, and apologia he published in 1937. Here he stated that his years as an officer of the Indian police had left him with "an immense weight of guilt that I had got to expiate." To do this he felt he needed "to submerge myself, to get right down among the oppressed, to be one of them and on their side against the tyrants" (247). If these statements, which for many years formed part of an unquestioned "Orwell mystique," now sound a trifle melodramatic, it is only fair to add what Orwell himself went on to say, that he "had at that time no interest in Socialism or any other economic theory," and that when he visualized the oppressed, "my mind turned immediately towards the extreme cases, the social outcasts: tramps, beggars, criminals, prostitutes," rather than to the working classes of

England. It is also worth noting that, apart from necessarily mentioning the place name as part of his first book's title, *Down and Out in Paris and London,* he related none of his "expiation" to the period of nearly two years, from early 1928 to late 1929, that he spent in Paris. The processes by which the Eric Blair of 1927 became the George Orwell of 1933, and by which the young writer in search of material became the committed, but still idiosyncratic, socialist were indirect, varied, and gradual; the second process took longer than the first.

For some years after 1927, Blair—still only a young man in his mid-twenties, for all his colonial "authority" and experience—found in his parents' house at Southwold a recurrent point of reference, a home in the sense defined by Robert Frost: "a place where, when you have to go there, they have to take you in."[2] But he could hardly stay there long, or use it as a writer's study; nor did he try to. With five months' salary (about two hundred pounds) saved from Burma, he first inquired about cheap lodgings in London. The poet Ruth Pitter, a family friend, found him a room on Portobello Road, in Notting Hill, where he painstakingly and awkwardly began to write; she described his first efforts as being "like a cow with a musket."[3] From there he made his first forays into the East End of London, the fringe and outcast world described by Jack London in *The People of the Abyss,* which he had read at school. In shabby clothes acquired for the purpose and bringing him an instant acceptance he welcomed, he stayed in a common lodging house in Limehouse, in London's dock area, and with scant concern for warmth or his poor state of health adopted the peripatetic routine of the destitute, moving from one tramps' hostel, or "spike," to another. This was the earliest of Blair's experiences to issue in publication: his dispassionate essay "The Spike" was accepted by the magazine *Adelphi* early in 1930 and appeared there under his own name in April 1931.

In the spring of 1928 Blair went to Paris, and stayed there until nearly the end of 1929. Little evidence of his life there survives, except for what he himself supplied: as late as 1946 in his essay "How the Poor Die," the result of two weeks he spent with pneumonia in the Cochin hospital in February 1929; and in 1933 in *Down and Out in Paris and London.* He avowed in 1937 that "nearly all the incidents" in *Down and Out* "actually happened" (*Wigan Pier,* 249), but the book makes it clear that what is narrated in chapters 3 to 23 covered at most the last six months of his Paris period, when most of his remaining money (no more than four pounds) was stolen, and he was obliged, for lack of English language pupils, to work as a dishwasher in a hotel on the Rue de Rivoli and later in a pretentious, bad, and short-lived restaurant.

Blair's poverty in Paris was thus late and accidental, rather than early and sought out, though when it came it deepened his sympathy for underdogs and wage-slaves, and caused him to expose in his writings the sordidness and desperation that lay behind the city's smart and prosperous facade. Yet given the reputation of Paris as a haven for expatriate writers—James Joyce, F. Scott Fitzgerald, Ernest Hemingway—it seems unnecessary to suppose that Blair went there for any other reason than to develop his talent in what would have been, for most of his time there, an attractive and lively environment. Paris was also the city in which his aunt Nelly Limouzin was living, and one that was not expensive, though the rate of exchange was less favorable than in 1926: 120 rather than 250 francs to the pound. In *Down and Out,* Blair described the area he had lived in as "quite a representative Paris slum," but it was not quite that.[4] Hemingway had earlier called the district around the Rue du Pot de Fer "the best part of the Latin Quarter," which suggests the Bohemian and the exotic rather than the grayly sordid.[5] Its inhabitants were, in fact, preponderantly migrant foreign workers rather than a downtrodden French proletariat.

Though Paris provided him with the material that later made up nearly two thirds of *Down and Out in Paris and London,* Blair did not manage to publish much while he was there. In his introduction to the French translation of that book, published in Paris in 1935, he spoke of having written two novels during his stay; what they were like is not known. Blair's first publication was a piece on censorship of the arts in England, which came out in *Le Monde;* he also published a few short articles in the radical journal *Le Progrès civique,* including one on imperialism in Burma. Blair's "outsider" stance as a purveyor of English matters to the French, in French, was reversed in his first piece to appear in England: a short essay describing the marketing of a new right-wing Paris newspaper, *L'Ami du peuple,* entitled "A Farthing Newspaper," which appeared at the end of December 1928 in *G. K.'s Weekly,* a paper run by G. K. Chesterton. But his attempt to place a number of short stories, through an agent of the McClure Newspaper Syndicate whom he met in Paris, were unsuccessful, though the agent praised his "very good powers of description."[6]

News of the availability of a job as private tutor to a backward boy in Walberswick, only a mile from Southwold, drew Blair out of his dishwasher's life and back to England, in time to spend Christmas of 1929 at his parents' home: now as, to all appearances, an unsuccessful writer rather than an unsuccessful policeman. Nevertheless, he was beginning to make more headway. From Paris, in August 1929, he had sent an early and longer version of "The Spike" to Max Plowman, literary editor of the *Adelphi,* the distinguished literary quarterly founded in 1923 by John Middleton Murry, and during 1930 he contributed a number of reviews to it, including one of J. B. Priestley's best-selling novel *Angel Pavement.* His own failure, so far, to produce even one publishable novel in no way inhibited the frankness of his criticism of Priestley's fourth, which seemed to him no more than "a competent and agreeable novel" by "a blatantly second-rate novelist."[7] What had clearly outraged Blair was the extravagant way in which others had compared Priestley to Dickens, a writer he venerated and on whom he was to write, nine years later, one of his best essays—and, indeed, one of the best essays ever written on Dickens. It is worth noting, at the beginning of Blair's review, a remark on an aspect of *Angel Pavement*'s subject matter that presages the left-wing humanitarianism of George Orwell: "Clerks are men and brothers, and fit material for art—applause, therefore, to the writer who can use them."

Blair's tutoring came to an end in the spring of 1930, and for much of the next two years he divided his time between writing about his previous experiences and tramping, which provided him with new material to be written up. His tramping, deliberately undertaken on a minimum of money, involved nights in "spikes" and nights "sleeping rough," and was done in the Home Counties around London. It was not, however, a total immersion; rather it was a sequence of separate plunges, made from the springboards of friends' houses: Ruth Pitter's studio in Notting Hill, the Chelsea apartment of Sir Richard Rees, a fellow Etonian who from 1930 was coeditor of the *Adelphi,* and the house in Golders Green of Mabel Fierz, a fellow contributor to the *Adelphi* whom he had first met in Southwold, and who was to prove instrumental in finding a publisher for *Down and Out in Paris and London.* In August and September 1931, Blair worked in the Kentish hopfields alongside the working-class people who regularly migrated there each year from the East End of London: he used his experiences there for part of *A Clergyman's Daughter* (1935), and it was the hop-pickers (akin to the migrant "Okies" of John Steinbeck's *The Grapes of Wrath*) who gave him the notion of the undefeatable "proles" that later provided an optimistic gleam beside the gray totalitarianism depicted in

Nineteen Eighty-Four. Around the end of 1931 Blair attempted to add one more experience to his willed identification with the underdog: that of being sent to prison. Unfortunately, contriving to get himself arrested in Whitechapel as "drunk and disorderly" procured him only a few hours "inside": for all his scruffy disguise as "Edward Burton," a variant of "P. S. Burton," the name he used when tramping, it would seem that the authorities recognized him as of a higher class than those they usually arrested. In August 1932 he wrote a description of his experiences, entitled "Clink," and made use of it in his third novel, *Keep the Aspidistra Flying* (1936).

Blair completed the first version of his Paris experiences by the end of 1930, and submitted it to the publishing firm of Jonathan Cape under the title "A Scullion's Diary." Cape found it too short (it was only thirty-five thousand words); but even when, at their suggestion, Blair expanded it, they still did not accept it. The expanded manuscript fared no better with Faber and Faber, to whom he sent it at the end of 1931. In February 1932 T. S. Eliot informed him that, though interesting, it was "decidedly too short," and went on to make a criticism that can still be leveled at the published book: "it seems to me too loosely constructed, as the French and English episodes fall into two parts with very little to connect them." Where Cape had not objected to "Paris," Eliot's final suggestion conveys a preference for "London": "you should have enough material from your experience to make a very interesting book on down-and-out life in England alone."[8]

Naturally discouraged, and feeling perhaps caught between two stools, Blair gave up on his manuscript at this point, leaving it with his friend Mabel Fierz and not caring what she did with it. He also began to wonder whether the continuation of a life of "utter poverty" would not become "self-defeating,"[9] and at Easter 1932 took up a post as head—and only—master at the "Hawthorns High School for Boys," a diminutive and undistinguished private school in Hayes, Middlesex, which prepared lower-middle-class boys for clerical jobs. He taught there, and at a somewhat better establishment in nearby Uxbridge, until the end of 1933, later making use of various of his experiences in his second novel, *A Clergyman's Daughter* (1935). While he was in Hayes he also managed to complete one hundred pages of his first novel, *Burmese Days.*

Meanwhile, due to the efforts of Mabel Fierz, his Paris/London manuscript had been read by a literary agent, Leonard Moore, submitted by Moore without Blair's knowledge to the left-wing publishing firm of Victor Gollancz, and accepted for publication. Gollancz's reader, the poet and reviewer Gerald Gould, had reported on it with great enthusiasm, calling it "an extraordinarily forceful and important social document," and thus anticipating what was to become the recurrent note in critical and popular response to "George Orwell": the sense of him as a courageous and truthful explorer of areas of human experience known at first hand to few of his contemporaries. Fearful of possible libel action, however, Gollancz insisted that Blair replace all the real place and personal names he had used. Gollancz wished to entitle the book "The Confessions of a Down-and-Out," a wish that in effect prevailed; but it provoked in Blair, for all his sympathy with those he had depicted, an oddly middle-class response: he "would rather answer to 'dishwasher' than to 'down-and-out,'" and preferred as titles either "The Lady Poverty" or "Confessions of a Dishwasher."[10]

Blair had his way in one matter, however. He told Leonard Moore that he was "not proud" of the book, and wished it to be "published pseudonymously."[11] Given his reason—whether or not one agrees with it—for wishing to adopt a pseudonym, not too much should be made of the actual pseudonym adopted, however much "George Orwell" has come to stand not only for an author but for an outlook, and to possess the ring of historical inevitability. At the time, the name offered simply a convenient anonymity: if *Down and Out* were unsuccessful, Eric Blair would not have to blush; conversely, if the book had any kind of success, "I can always use the same pseudonym again."[12] In putting forward to Gollancz, via Leonard Moore, his preference for the pseudonym "George Orwell" (the "George" stolidly English, the "Orwell" the name of a Suffolk river thirty miles from Southwold), he also suggested "P. S. Burton," a name that would have been recognizable by his tramping associates, "Kenneth Miles," which sounded forthright and soldierly, and the comically pompous "H. Lewis Allways,"[13] a name possibly modeled on that of such a writer as H. Seton Merriman. It was Gollancz's agreement to "George Orwell" that turned personal whim into public image, together with Blair's retention of the name as a familiar identifier on subsequent works of fiction, documentation, and polemic. Yet for two melancholy and romantic poems published in the *Adelphi* in March 1934 Blair used the name he was born with. Nor did he ever legally abandon it, keeping it for his business dealings and for letters to his family and to many friends; and it is the name that was carved on his gravestone. "George Orwell" was not, then, a repudiation of Eric Blair; yet since it is as George Orwell that, in 1933, he emerged into ever-widening public notice, it is proper that he should be so referred to from this point on.

Down and Out in Paris and London (1933)

Orwell's first book appeared in London in January 1933. His struggle into significant authorship had taken more than five years, and he was almost thirty; but at least the long haul did not topple into anticlimax. *Down and Out in Paris and London* sold rapidly enough to figure in the *Sunday Times*'s list of "best sellers of the week,"[14] and when an American edition was published a few months later, its dust jacket bore some phrases of commendation from J. B. Priestley, more generous to Orwell than Orwell had been to him. "Uncommonly good reading," the famous novelist pronounced it, "an excellent book and a valuable social document."[15]

There is no doubt of the book's value as a social document. W. H. Davies, the "tramp poet" who had published *The Autobiography of a Super Tramp* twenty-five years earlier, reviewed the "extraordinary confessions" and authoritatively assured their author that they were "packed with unique and strange information"; he also supplemented Orwell's disquisition on London street slang (chap. 32) with his own examples.[16] The comments of reviewers, both British and American, make clear how interesting Orwell's material was to his contemporaries, and how well his choice of topic chimed in with the social consciousness of the 1930s.

But if one expects the term to convey more than a vague gesture of praise, and to mean a work that has unity of conception and structure, one can hardly agree with Priestley's description of *Down and Out* as an "excellent book." "A Scullion's Diary," confined entirely to Paris, had seemed too short and slight to Jonathan Cape, but its expansion by more than 50 percent grafted on to it material of a very different kind, the change of location being only one aspect of this difference. Taken by itself, the English material would also have been too short to suit a publisher, and though "thicker" in its presentation—more densely detailed and closer to home—it is also grayer, unleavened by exotic incidents and unmitigated by the slight sense of unreality that accompanies the depiction of foreign experience.

The difference in "feel" between Orwell's Paris and his London is suggested by two of his remarks. Describing the local bistro in chapter 2, he comments: "I wish one could find a pub in London a quarter as cheery"; when back in London in chapter 25 he registers his environment as "so much cleaner and quieter and drearier." However low his financial level when he experienced it, he still found Paris a place of "wine, women and song."[17] Orwell describes even starvation in terms of Baudelaire's "jeune squelette" (chap. 3), and the quotation from Ernest Dowson relates aptly to chapter 2, which—much to the pre-publication disquiet of Victor Gollancz[18]—details in "decadent" fashion the rape of a helpless young girl in the all-red room of a brothel. From Paris picturesque the book moves to London sociological, to the world of the deceived folk-song heroine "O Unhappy Bella" (chap. 34), "tea and two slices," and the tramps, "ordinary human beings" whose plight is exacerbated by their separation from women (chap. 36). The transition from one world to the other, in chapter 24, is accomplished by means of a falsification. In reality, Orwell went straight from Paris to spend Christmas with his parents in Southwold and to tutor a backward boy there. In the book, he arrives in London to find his promised job delayed for a month, which "obliges" him to enter immediately the world of down-and-outs that in reality he had already experienced before Paris, and experienced again after his tutoring at Southwold ended. The reorganization yokes the different experiences more closely together by omitting the interval as irrelevant; it also has the advantage for Orwell of maintaining his authorial stance as a lone outsider, his relatives and friends in both Paris and England firmly relegated beyond the margins of his book.

According to his biographer, Bernard Crick, Orwell "was in two minds whether *Down and Out* was journalism or literature."[19] Gallimard, who brought out a French translation in 1935 under the title *La Vache enragée,* had no doubt it belonged to the latter category, even pronouncing it in firm capitals on the cover: ROMAN. To call it a novel was extraordinary, in view of Orwell's specially supplied introduction, which made it quite clear that the book described real places and events, even if the people in it were intended as "representative types" rather than as individuals[20]—a perhaps disingenuous assertion that is decidedly not borne out by the vivid and detailed portraits of Boris the ex-convict officer, Paddy Jacques the Irish tramp, and Bozo the London pavement artist. The book has nothing approaching a plot, and even if one describes its narrative as "picaresque" there are still "sociological" passages to account for: the careful analysis of staff hierarchy at the "Hotel X" (chap. 13), the lists of London slang words (chap. 32), and the chapters (22 and 36) devoted to general discussion of the lives of *plongeurs* and tramps and how their lives relate to society at large. But perhaps Gallimard was even more wary of libel actions than Gollancz: certainly the book's publication in London provoked within a month an indignant letter to the *Times* from an experienced Paris restaurateur, and a protest in the *Licensed Victuallers Gazette.*[21]

It is best to take the book as a documentary, shading from sinful rose to institutional gray. This seems obvious enough now, when "documentary" is a genre familiar from books, journalism, and television: a sort of alternation between the particular observing eye and "the way things are," in which our interest fluctuates between the commentator's personality, which is partly revealed by the choice of material, and an external reality that imposes on us as having an objective existence. The genre was less familiar in 1933, however, and Orwell may be counted among its pioneers.

"Poverty is what I am writing about," he declares squarely in chapter 1, and indeed he presents a wide-ranging picture of it: his own, which was temporary, and the various sorts of poverty more fully and permanently experienced by those with whom he came into contact. His depiction of his own is by turns unemphatic, wry, and buoyant. "Your first contact with poverty" is not "terrible . . . merely squalid and boring," he says in the first chapter; adding in chapter 2 that it "annihilates the future . . . the less money you have, the less you worry." And despite the middle-class squeamishness it initially provoked in him—the inability to tell a shop assistant that he could afford precisely one franc's worth of bread, the pouring away of his last half-litre of milk because a bedbug fell in it (chap. 3)—he was able to adjust rapidly to his new state: "You have talked so often of going to the dogs—and well, here are the dogs, and you have reached them, and you can stand it. It takes off a lot of anxiety." However forcefully he later recollects his unhappiness at St. Cyprian's in "Such, Such were the Joys," its capricious and spartan regime had clearly prepared him for coping courageously and resourcefully with adversity.

It would be inaccurate to call Orwell a "compassionate" writer. Though himself beaten at St. Cyprian's and at Eton, he did not, when a schoolmaster in Hayes, become a kind of educational pacifist: he was friendly, sharing his interests with the boys and taking them for informative country walks, but he did not hesitate to use the cane, and according to one of his pupils he "hit hard."[22] In the description of his own poverty in Paris and London his tone totally lacks self-pity, and in the description of others' poverty, his resentment on their behalf never gets the better of his close observation. In many parts of the book the latter—for example, his detailing of how the Paris hotel worked, his catalogue of the various types of sleeping accommodation available for tramps (chap. 27), his interpolated anecdotes about Parisian "characters" like Roucolle the miser (chap. 23)—seems to function independently, as padding, as quasi-official reporting, or as irrepressible personal interest. Typical of Orwell's temperament is his remark about his life in the hotel when he was learning the job: "For curiosity I counted the number of times I was called *maquereau* [pimp] during the day, and it was thirty-nine" (chap. 10).

Orwell is sympathetic, but he is not sentimental. Of Paddy Jacques, for instance, though he calls him a "good fellow" and concludes that "it was malnutrition and not any native vice that had destroyed his manhood," he also says that "he had the regular character of a tramp—abject, envious, a jackal's character" (chap. 28). Though he points out the degradation of tramp life, cold, hunger, enforced idleness, being preached at by clergymen in exchange for charity and restricted by narrow Salvation Army rules from harmless pastimes like card-playing, he cannot help reporting the dirt that accompanies it: the scene in the bathroom at the spike at "Romton" was "extraordinarily repulsive" (chap. 27). His chapters of general comment on the lives of *plongeurs,* beggars, and tramps do not exploit a presumed middle-class guilt or trade in the rhetoric of universal brotherhood, rather they try to correct misconceptions and question assumptions. Why is it necessary for people to work a fourteen-hour day for four pounds a month in "inferno" conditions, merely to provide unnecessary and often delusive "luxuries"? Why the universal contempt for beggars, who are not people who have "sold [their] honour" but merely unfortunates who have "made the mistake of choosing a trade at which it is impossible to grow rich" (chap. 31)? Why should down-and-outs be forced into nomadism, moving on each day from spike to spike, when they could stay longer and be more self-supporting, growing their own food and doing useful work that might restore their self-respect?

In posing such questions, Orwell moves from observer and participant to social commentator and would-be reformer. The last, however, only raises its head tentatively: the almost identical phrases with which two of these chapters begin ("I want to give my opinions about the life of a Paris *plongeur*" [22]; "I want to set down some general remarks about tramps" [36]) seem casual, random, even clumsy, rather than sly and disarming, the quiet prelude to a devastating barrage. The "vocabulary" chapter opens with the same tentativeness: "I want to put in some notes, as short as possible, on London slang and swearing." The note of apology here adds to the impression that Orwell was frequently unsure whether his material, which clearly interested him, would interest his readers, and whether all the various elements of it belonged together in one book. But if, like Harriet Beecher Stowe's Topsy, *Down and Out* "just growed," it does not lack interest: Orwell's concern ensures this, as does his rapid though not polished style whose veracity is not impaired by the occasional lively exaggeration.

Much of the material in the book has naturally dated. The postwar British welfare state has significantly reduced the number of tramps, labor-saving devices have cut down the wear and tear of hotel work, and one may at least hope that "disgusting filth" (chap. 12) is no longer only a double door away from a spotless hotel dining room. Such dating would not have bothered Orwell: "as though every book worth reading didn't date!" he wrote to Henry Miller in 1936.[23] To know that life was once "like this," to know that someone cared enough to describe it, and to have it so deftly and fully described that it is preserved is enough to support *Down and Out*'s claim to be "literature."

Interestingly, Orwell himself, writing to his agent Leonard Moore in 1932, spoke of chapter 2, Charlie's description of having the girl in the Paris brothel as "about the only good bit of writing in the book."[24] The room where the incident occurs is described as "a heavy, stifling red, as though the light were shining through bowls of blood," and the section concludes: "All my savagery, my passion, were scattered like the petals of a rose, . . . I was left cold and languid, full of vain regrets." Orwell's judgment suggests the mixed aims and nature of his book, but it is not for such an uninspired, 1890s-ish passage that the modern reader will value it. Instead one responds to Orwell's vicarious pride in the efficiency of Mario, the indefatigable Italian *cafetier* (chap. 11), to the "vast capacities for hope" in Boris, the lame but ebullient Russian émigré who worked alongside Orwell at the "Hotel X" and the pretentious "Auberge de Jehan Cottard' with its "two large rats sitting on the kitchen table" (chap. 19); and to Bozo the pavement artist, also lame, the indomitable "exceptional man" who watched for meteors and felt that "rich or poor, all was well as long as one could say 'I'm a free man in *here*,'" in the mind (chap. 30). One responds, that is, to Orwell's depiction not only of human misery but also of human dignity and of the human ability, in the words of William Faulkner in his speech accepting the Nobel Prize, not only to endure but to prevail. A general remark on Orwell's work made by Christopher Sykes in 1950 applies with particular force to *Down and Out in Paris and London*: "His themes are usually distressing, but somehow his valiant treatment of them sends our spirits up."[25]

Burmese Days (1934)

What Orwell wanted to be at this period of his life, however, was not a writer of documentaries but a novelist. According to Bernard Crick he began or resumed work on *Burmese Days,* [26] his first novel, in October 1930; but his main concentration on it came in 1932 and 1933, when he was teaching in Hayes. "The longness and complicatedness are horrible," he wrote to his friend Eleanor Jaques on 19 October 1932.[27] By the beginning of 1933 he had sent the first hundred pages to his agent, hoping that its rarity as a novel set in Burma might "offset the lack of action in the story."[28] The remainder of the novel, finished by 1933, remedied the lack of action by means of murder, a native riot, and a suicide. *Burmese Days* is, in fact, packed with incident and atmospheric detail and perhaps the richest of all Orwell's novels, the record not only of disenchantment with colonialism but of a powerful if ambivalent involvement with the country in which he had spent five impressionable years, and which, clearly, he had had to get out of his system.

Orwell's own feelings about the novel were mixed. In 1933 he was satisfied neither with its rendering nor with its "fearful length—about Priestley-size."[29] It is, by a small margin, the longest of Orwell's novels, but not at all comparable in length to the two mammoth novels by Priestley, *The Good Companions* (1929) and *Angel Pavement* (1930), of which he was disparagingly thinking. Even when he saw the novel in proof, in the summer of 1934, it "made me spew" and he felt like rewriting "large chunks" of it.[30] By this point it had been rejected by Victor Gollancz, who feared libel suits as Orwell had not bothered to change real people's names, and also by Heinemann and Cape. The novel was finally published, without alteration, in the United States by Harpers in October 1934 and sold thirty-five hundred copies. The British edition, brought out by Gollancz in June 1935 after extensive legal consultations, contained a number of name changes: the Burmese official U Po Kyin became U Po Sing, the hero's friend Veraswami became Murkhaswami, and the Lackersteens (possibly modeled on Orwell's relatives in Moulmein, the Limouzins) became the Latimers.

Critical response to the novel in England was largely favorable. Cyril Connolly, whom Orwell had not seen since their days at Eton, called it in the *New Statesman* "an admirable novel"; the anthropologist Geoffrey Gorer, in a letter to Orwell, described it as "an absolutely admirable statement of fact told as vividly and with as little bitterness as possible"; and G. W. Stonier, reviewing it in the *Fortnightly,* stated that the "isolation of Burma" was "caught with glaring realism."[31] In August 1936, having by that time published four books, Orwell referred to *Burmese Days* in a letter to Henry Miller as "the only one of my books that I am pleased with," though it was only the "descriptions of scenery" that he valued.[32]

Descriptions of scenery are not what spring to mind as the most characteristic element in Orwell's novels. Orwell is a writer with opinions, ideals, prejudices; his feelings are oriented toward human beings rather than away from them. On the rare occasions in his later novels where landscapes figure, such as when Gordon Comstock and Rosemary visit Burnham Beeches in *Keep the Aspidistra Flying* and when Winston and Julia make love in a glade "misty with bluebells" (*Nineteen Eighty-Four*), nature provides a momentary escape from societal pressures, opportunity for uncomplicated human happiness. It does this also in *Coming Up for Air*; but though this novel is essentially an elegy for the vanished England of Orwell's boyhood, its forthright narrator George Bowling lacks the poetry that would convey the natural beauty of the past in a conventionally elegiac way. *Burmese Days,* though it offers many opinions with an authorial obtrusiveness that Orwell does not seem to have thought a fault,[33] is a rather different novel from the others. The poetic quality in it suggests that the Burmese landscape had been too exotic and breathtaking for him to resist, and had drawn from him an eloquent recognition of the independent existence of natural beauty.

He himself, in his essay of 1946, "Why I Write," acknowledged *Burmese Days* as conforming to his earliest notion of the sort of books he wanted to write: "enormous naturalistic novels with unhappy endings, full of detailed descriptions and arresting similes, and also full of purple passages in which words were used partly for the sake of their sound."[34] At the time Orwell wrote *Burmese Days* he was still publishing poems. He wrote few after 1936, the year from which he dated the assumption by his work of a preeminent political purpose, and by 1946 he was dismissive of books of any but a "political" kind: "I can see that it was only where I lacked a *political* purpose that I wrote lifeless books and was betrayed into purple passages, sentences without meaning, decorative adjectives and humbug generally."[35]

It is necessary to defend *Burmese Days,* the testament of Eric Blair, against the implied sneers of his "born again" successor. *Burmese Days* is far from being a lifeless book, and this is not merely because its seething irritation with British imperialism displays political "purpose." It is also because of the beauty and sensitivity of its descriptive writing, the very element that the younger Orwell singled out for praise in his letter to Henry Miller. No "cow with a musket" could have achieved the distinction of Orwell's brief description of moonlight in chapter 15: "The light lay thick, as though palpable, on everything, crusting the earth and the rough bark of trees like some dazzling salt, and every leaf seemed to bear a freight of solid light, like snow."[36] Even better, breaking through into genuinely poetic illumination, is his description of the book's main character in a rare moment of happiness, looking up into a peepul tree full of green pigeons: "Flory gazed up into the great green dome of the tree, trying to distinguish the birds; they were invisible, they matched the leaves so perfectly, and yet the whole tree was alive with them, shimmering, as though the ghosts of birds were shaking it." It is not only where it possesses a political purpose that prose can satisfy Orwell's famous requirement that it be "like a window pane."[37]

There is a further reason for the vitality of *Burmese Days*: it is, simply, a powerful and involving story, with an "unhappy ending," about an individual—a description that applies to only one other novel by Orwell, *Nineteen Eighty-Four.* All Orwell's novels employing human characters have in common the fact that their protagonists are, or become, estranged from their societies; but it is only in these two that the reader's sympathies are sharply engaged on their behalf and truly feel their isolation and disappointments. In *Burmese Days,* however, the reader's identification with the main character, John Flory, is less complete than it is with Winston Smith: in totalitarian Oceania social conformity is the price of physical survival, but in colonial Burma it is merely the price of peer approval. This difference allows the reader, and author, of *Burmese Days* some scope for criticism of Flory and for a less than total condemnation of the system.

Orwell presents his main character in chapters 2 through 5, describing both his current circumstances as a thirty-five-year-old manager for a British timber company, working near the small administrative center of Kyauktada in Upper Burma, and the previous pattern of life that has led to the present situation and made it virtually inescapable. Though "not ill made," Flory has one feature that leaps to the eye: a "hideous" dark blue birthmark on his left cheek. Though this plays a small physical role in the novel, increasing Flory's self-consciousness and reducing his self-esteem, its true function is symbolic; it is the mark of Cain, signifying Flory's mental difference from his British compatriots, whom he sees as philistine and bigoted, "dull boozing witless porkers" talking "evil-minded drivel" in their determinedly whites-only club. Flory's closest friend (a touch that inevitably brings to mind Forster's *A Passage to India* [1924]) is the Indian doctor Veraswami, who holds the official post of Civil Surgeon and Superintendent of the local jail. Ironically, Veraswami is intensely pro-British, seeing Britons as superior beings and bringers of civilization; but in his company Flory can let off steam about what he derides as "Pox Britannica," an exploitative imperialism hiding underneath "white man's burden humbug" (chap. 3).

In such details as making Flory a decade older than he was himself when he left Burma, and in giving him the background of only a minor public school, Orwell distances himself from his protagonist, whom he depicts as sharing some of his compatriots' colonial habits and assumptions: when in Kyauktada, Flory goes to the club most evenings, "to play bridge and get three parts drunk" (chap. 4); and, as he frankly tells Veraswami, "I don't want the Burmans to drive me out of this country. God forbid! I'm here to make money, like everybody else" (chap. 3). When speaking in his authorial voice, Orwell tries to avoid simplistic anticolonialism. The bigoted Ellis, who calls Flory "Booker Washington, the niggers' pal," is "one of those Englishmen . . . who should never be allowed to set foot in the East"; but he is also "an intelligent man and an able servant of his firm" (chap. 3). The local resident, Mr. Macgregor, is depicted as in the main a good man. Though his paternalism stops short of wishing the Burmese to be free, he is "deeply fond of them" and "it always pained him to see them wantonly insulted" (chap. 2). Orwell's brief vignette on police methods in chapter 6 places the brutal directness of a Burmese sub-Inspector side by side with the pained aversion of the British police superintendent, hostile to dacoits (bandits) and rebels but not to "those poor devils of common thieves." While not approving of the system itself, Orwell is far from condemning the British who operate it, and even expresses sympathy for them. "You could forgive the Europeans a great deal of their bitterness. Living among Orientals would try the patience of a saint" (chap. 2).

For all the irritation expressed by Flory, it would be inaccurate to read *Burmese Days* as an antiimperialist tract by its creator. The only corrupt official is a Burmese, the immensely fat and bribe-rich magistrate U Po Kyin, whose detached malignity and devious cunning determine much of the novel's action, and whose ambition to be the single "show" Oriental elected to the Kyauktada club leads finally to the defeat and demotion of Veraswami, and the destruction of Flory's precarious last chance at happiness. Though U Po Kyin himself dies suddenly at the end of the novel, before he can build the pagoda that will atone for his sins and ensure his reincarnation in human form, his remote control of events, and the fact that it is he whom Orwell chooses to introduce to the reader first, suggest that Burma, united under British rule as recently as 1888, can take care of itself. It remains, in its essential mystery, beyond British jurisdiction, and thus reduces the "question" of imperialism to a minor issue.

In fact, though Orwell does not emphasize this, *Burmese Days* possesses an enlarging "Chinese box" structure. At the center are the English "rulers," including Flory. Surrounding them are the Burmese "ruled," who in the scheming person of U Po Kyin are really in control; enclosing all is an ironic, Hardyesque fate, which carries off Flory and U Po Kyin alike in death, and, in the novel's final words, translates Elizabeth Lackersteen from a pretty if shallow young woman into "the position for which Nature had designed her from the first, that of a burra memsahib."

The novel's last three pages—in which after Flory's death all loose ends are tied up—have a hard-boiled, slightly cynical evenhandedness, a sourish "happy-ever-after" quality, that recalls the stories of W. Somerset Maugham.[38] Orwell valued them so much that he stoutly resisted his American publishers' wish that they be cut: "I hate a novel in which the principal characters are not disposed of at the end."[39] Nevertheless it is the confused, thwarted feelings of Flory, to which this authorial dispassion stands in stark contrast, that are the most powerful element in *Burmese Days,* and the one in which the character of Orwell himself can be most clearly inferred, though not the precise details of his Burmese experience. Flory, who has spent fifteen years in Burma, suggests a portrait, both sympathetic and horrified, of what Orwell suspected he might have become had he stayed longer than five. Like Orwell a dissenter among conformists, he is also the first depiction—to recur in Gordon Comstock and Winston Smith—of one whose rebellion is the more intense for harboring within it a temptation, even a need, to acknowledge authority, to "love Big Brother."

Flory's essential problem is his isolation, which after fifteen years in Burma has become unbearable. Though he is shown as efficient at his job, a good shot, and resourceful in a crisis like the native riot in chapter 22, he also reads books, responds with interest and pleasure to many aspects of Burmese life and landscape, and finds it more and more of a burden to lead "a life of lies" and keep his detestation of the "pukka sahib" mentality to himself. Yet, most of the time, it is as hard for him to rebel as it is to conform: guiltily suppressing his better nature, he acquiesces in the bigotry around him and it is not until chapter 21 that he summons up the moral courage to propose his friend Veraswami for membership in the club. In a phrase that brings D. H. Lawrence to mind, Orwell shrewdly pinpoints the ambivalence of Flory's feelings, and the temptation he is exposed to: "it is a corrupting thing to live one's real life in secret. One should live with the stream of life, not against it" (chap. 5).

Burma has provided Flory with "a good life while one was young and need not think about the future or the past" (chap. 5). Recalled there, at thirty, while on the way to his one and only leave in England, he has recognized that "he was glad to be coming back" to what is now his true "native country, his home." But this recognition is accompanied by the sense of "a vast change and deterioration" in his life. If Flory dislikes his British compatriots, no more is he completely assimilated into Burma. The company of his young Burmese mistress, Ma Hla May ("Miss Pretty"), offers him no real companionship, and what was once sexual pleasure now brings only self-contempt. Though the Burmese landscape is still beautiful to him, it is incomplete by itself. What Flory needs, he decides, is a "quite impossible she": someone who "would love Burma as he loved it and hate it as he hated it. . . . Someone who understood him: a friend, that was what it came down to" (chap. 5).

Unfortunately, the young English girl with whom he proceeds to fall in love is precisely a "quite impossible she" for Flory, just as he is the wrong man for her. Eton-cropped, "faintly coloured like an apple-blossom," Elizabeth Lackersteen is physically the ideal 1920s girl. In her use of words like "adore" and "divine," the reader quickly perceives her superficiality; but she seems infinitely romantic to Flory, having come out to stay with relatives after a period in Paris, which he imagines her to have spent "sitting in cafés with foreign art students, drinking white wine and talking about Marcel Proust" (chap. 6). But just as her initial friendliness to Flory stems from her overestimating his courage when he "saves" her from a harmless water buffalo, so his view of her is based on a misconception of her mind, which Orwell corrects in an authorial flashback in chapter 7. Her time in Paris, spent in reduced circumstances with a widowed mother who has taken up a squalid pseudoartistic life, has not unreasonably made her recoil from mess and "sordid meanness." She loathes the very word "Art," and longs with a half-repellent, half-pathetic snobbishness for the "lovely, lovely golden world" of English upper-class life, of which in richer days she has had a taste as a boarder at an expensive girls' school. More than anything else, Elizabeth values the conventional, and Flory's naive, enthusiastic attempts to interest her in local life, by taking her to visit the bazaar (chap. 11) and to see the *pwe,* the Burmese native entertainment (chap. 8), simply backfire, spoiling her view of him as a "manly man." The lack of aesthetic rapport between them is captured in her response to his lyrical description of the graceful *pwe*-dancer: it was "almost, she thought bitterly, as though he were quoting poetry!"

Dogs, gramophone records, tennis: ruefully Flory comes to realize (chap. 11) that "trash" topics like these are what Elizabeth prefers, but it makes no difference to his feelings. In chapter 14, however, when they go shooting in the jungle, both are in their element, Flory the competent instructor, Elizabeth the eager and admiring neophyte. When Elizabeth shoots a sitting green pigeon, "she was conscious of an extraordinary desire to fling her arms round Flory's neck and kiss him; and in some way it was the killing of the pigeon that made her feel this." And when, later, Flory shoots a leopard and Elizabeth keeps her nerve, an unspoken compact is created between them. The whole episode, mixing lyrical description with a tacit, Lawrentian awareness of the close tie between death and sex, culminates in a phrase that conveys not only the momentary unison of Flory and Elizabeth, but the value that Orwell, himself not simply an aesthete and intellectual, attached to physical activity: "They were happy with that inordinate happiness that comes of exhaustion and achievement, and with which nothing else in life—no joy of either the body or the mind—is even able to be compared." Yet when, at the club (chap. 15), Flory at last kisses Elizabeth, he fails to follow through with the proposal of marriage she by now expects, and instead, wishing to make her "understand," launches into an impassioned speech about the loneliness and pain of exile.

What chance Flory has is progressively destroyed by a combination of circumstances and character, plot and fate, which is too intricate to summarize adequately, but which Orwell handles with considerable skill. The arrival on police duty of Verrall, the arrogant, titled, ruthless young lieutenant, whom Orwell describes not without sardonic admiration, excites all Elizabeth's romanticism and snobbery, and Flory suffers agonies of sexual jealousy together with totally ineffectual self-loathing. When Elizabeth and Verrall dance, they move "in perfect unison like some single animal," and "their fresh faces" are "unmarred in the pitiless light" (chap. 18). Verrall detests books, and with him she can be at one in unreflective physical activity: he even allows her to ride Belinda, his prized Arab mare. Nevertheless, though "a peach, by Christ!" to the normally austere Verrall, Elizabeth can no more succeed with him than Flory has with her: when the native uprising is quelled, Verrall decamps for Mandalay, leaving her and his local debts behind.

Yet even Verrall's departure, and Flory's own recent prestige as a result of his quick action during the riot, avail Flory nothing. Indeed, it is the prestige that ruins him: U Po Kyin must now intervene drastically to prevent the likely election of Flory's protégé Veraswami. For some time Flory's discarded mistress Ma Hla May has been bothering him in public for money, almost as if "someone else were egging her on" (chap. 17). The "someone" is U Po Kyin. Finally she interrupts a church service, screeching at Flory and tearing his clothes in "the last insult of a base-born Burmese woman" (chap. 24). Elizabeth is turned totally against Flory, partly by acute embarrassment at the scene, partly by the revelation of "his ugliness at this moment," the disfigurement of his birth mark, and all the "outsider"-ness that it embodies. His desperate attempts to explain, and his abject pleadings, only strengthen in her an instinctive aversion that is "deeper than reason or even self-interest." The intensity of Flory's infatuation, so finally rejected by its object, can only recoil on Flory himself; as if realizing that there is now nowhere and no one in the world to assuage his loneliness, he goes straight home and shoots himself.

Cyril Connolly, in his *New Statesman* review of *Burmese Days,* stated that "the author lacks the depth of Mr. E. M. Forster and the detachment of Mr. Somerset Maugham." The judgment is a true one, but was not meant by Connolly as a denigration, and it is not. Orwell was younger when he wrote *Burmese Days* than the Forster of *A Passage to India,* and one does not expect wisdom and profundity from a younger author. He spent longer in Burma than Maugham had in the various Southeast Asian ports of call where he set many of his finest stories, so one does not expect, or indeed want, detachment. Orwell's presentation of the Burmese political situation is many-sided, both emotional and intelligent, his description of the landscape vivid and evocative, his rendering of character always credible and often very penetrating. Flory is a particularly notable achievement, having in him many of Orwell's own traits, including dissent and a sense of inadequacy, but nevertheless completely convincing in his fictional context. Nor is Elizabeth a mere one-dimensional foil for him, but a character seen from within, vulnerable as well as detestable, and convincing in either aspect. She, too, has elements of Orwell in her. The two characters' moments of closeness are not difficult to credit, and the scenes of tension and disagreement between them have an involving force and immediacy.

Orwell's ability to convey eagerness, embarrassment, desire, and desperation is especially noticeable in *Burmese Days*; this may spring partly from the fact that, during its composition, he was conducting a not completely satisfactory affair with Eleanor Jaques, who shortly after married someone else. But whatever its autobiographical elements, *Burmese Days* is preeminently an accomplished work of fiction, not only re-creating a Burma the reader knows to have existed, but creating a complex world of characters and relationships that one comes to believe in. Indeed, if one disqualifies from competition *Animal Farm* on the grounds that it is an allegory, and *Nineteen Eighty-Four* because it is set in "the future," *Burmese Days* is undoubtedly Orwell's best novel.

Chapter Three
An English Novelist in the 1930s

Orwell's career as a schoolmaster came to an end in December 1933. His first school, the Hawthorns, having encountered financial difficulties and been sold by its owner, Orwell began the new academic year at a larger and better institution, Frays College in nearby Uxbridge. In December, however, he caught a chill that developed into a serious case of pneumonia. After some time in Uxbridge Cottage Hospital, he returned to his parents' home in Southwold early in 1934 to recuperate. He stayed there for ten months, the longest uninterrupted period he had spent at Southwold since 1922 when he had been preparing for the India Office examinations.

It was to be, in fact, his last sojourn in such a small town bastion of the English class system, and the novel he wrote there from April 1934 onwards, *A Clergyman's Daughter,* is in part an examination, irritated, often depressing, but not totally unsympathetic, of that stratified provincial environment. Orwell's later novels of the 1930s, *Keep the Aspidistra Flying* and *Coming Up for Air,* extend his depiction to other contemporary urban milieus: metropolitan and literary London, as experienced by an aspiring writer; and the suburban London of the lower-middle-class commuter. Yet while collectively the three novels are very much an Englishman's social commentary on the state of his country, each one has an individual theme, of great personal concern to its author, to which it is more deeply committed. In summary terms these themes may respectively be expressed as the loss of religious faith; the struggle for an acceptable modus vivendi in a world ruled by money; and the displacement of an ideal, semirural past by "progress" and the approach of war. Like John Flory, the protagonists of these three later novels are faced with the question of where in the world, and in their minds, to live. Unlike him, they are able to find an answer, or to soldier on.

A Clergyman's Daughter (1935)

A Clergyman's Daughter was Orwell's first novel to be published in England, in March 1935, anticipating *Burmese Days* by three months. It sold respectably, four thousand copies, but received mixed reviews. The novelist L. P. Hartley wrote of its "sure and bold treatment,"[1] but his view was expressed too unspecifically to carry weight, and it was not shared. Peter Quennell was nearer the mark in calling the novel "ambitious, but not entirely successful."[2] In its picaresque fashion it covers a fairly wide range of events and environments that are of interest in themselves, but Orwell's impatience with the strict necessities of fiction causes him to be unselective; much that is presented is not essential to the development of his main character, whom Quennell criticizes as "a literary abstraction to whom things happen."

As often after a long struggle (in this case, six months of relatively uninterrupted work) to express an originally "good idea," Orwell sent the novel to his agent, in October 1934, feeling he had "made a muck of it."[3] But, for a man so definite and positive when expressing opinions about life in nonfictional prose, Orwell was curiously nervous, debunking, and even savage when talking of his novels. It is hard to know whether this stemmed from modesty, a wish to disarm criticism, objective artistic judgment, an exhausted reaction after imaginative effort, or perhaps the fear that he had revealed too much of himself. When he told Brenda Salkeld, a physical education teacher and ex-clergyman's daughter[4] whom he had "employed . . . as a collaborator in two places,"[5] that the novel was "tripe," he was probably simply indulging in obligatory British unpretentiousness as friend to friend. Certainly the novel does not deserve such a swingeing, schoolboy dismissal. When in a letter to Henry Miller he called it "bollox,"[6] one may suspect, deeper than the wish to sound hard-boiled to an American writer he admired, an anxiety to play down the book's serious concern with religious belief before someone who would not have been interested in it. The letter, too, was written in 1936, the year in which Orwell became committed to the cause of democratic socialism, thus solving for himself the problem of belief that Dorothy Hare is left to cope with at the end of *A Clergyman's Daughter.*

"Bollox," the result of Orwell's hindsight of 1936, is too harsh a judgment on the book. The contemporary reader of Orwell, however, who is likely to approach him by way of his late and more well-known work, especially *Animal Farm* and *Nineteen Eighty-four,* may well find the religious, indeed the ecclesiastical, ambience of *A Clergyman's Daughter* a surprise, having formed the impression that Orwell is exclusively a secular writer. He usually is, and in fact much of Dorothy Hare's experience in *A Clergyman's Daughter* occurs in environments from which the notion of God is entirely absent. One could make no case for Orwell as a committed Christian; nevertheless he had been confirmed an Anglican, the need for faith (of whatever kind) was something he understood and sympathized with, and when working in suburban Hayes and living in provincial Southwold he was well aware not only of the Church as a symbol of belief but of churches as physical entities, where people went to worship.

It is not only that the realistic novelist in Orwell recognized the fictional potential of the Anglican church's place in the life of his country, and saw the religious impulse as an aspect of human character that needed to be given, at least once, its proper emphasis among other aspects. His choice of a country town parish and its rectory as a setting, and of such a person as a clergyman's daughter as a main character, is based on more than a thrifty writer's reluctance to let any of his observation of life go to waste. It stems particularly from a personal involvement with Anglicanism in 1932, and from a sense of himself, in 1932 and 1933, as someone becalmed between past and future and having no clear notion of what to believe in. "Faith vanishes, but the need for faith remains the same as before," Dorothy Hare reflects just before the end of *A Clergyman's Daughter.*[7] For Orwell the novel represents an attempt to treat the specifically religious aspect of this "need for faith" with seriousness and respect, to show its unsatisfactoriness for himself as an individual, and to put it behind him as a writer.

The sympathy with which Orwell enters into the Christian life of Dorothy Hare in the novel's first long section, and the unexpected familiarity he displays there with such matters as church ritual and theological controversy result from his paradoxical reaction, in 1932, to the fact that suburban Hayes was "one of the most god-forsaken places I ever struck."[8] He became friendly with the local High Anglican curate, a socialist, and as a result not only started attending church services but also acted twice a week as server at Holy Communion.[9] It is not clear whether he himself communicated: "I am afraid the bread might choke me," he wrote to Eleanor Jaques.[10] He read the Anglican *Church Times* regularly, being glad "to see that there is life in the old dog yet—I mean the poor old C of E." Notwithstanding Orwell's characteristic "jokey" tone, all this argues a degree of genuine interest and scrupulosity. He also, in June 1932, reviewed Karl Adam's *The Spirit of Catholicism,* far from dismissively;[11] and later that year he read *Belief in God* by Bishop Gore of Oxford, who had confirmed him at Eton: he found it "quite sound doctrine."[12] He had not put his church interests entirely behind him by the time he moved to Southwold in 1934: having promised to grow a vegetable marrow for the church's harvest festival in Hayes, he did the same in Southwold, producing an "enormous" one "which he'd fattened up"[13] just like Toagis in the imaginary Suffolk town of Knype Hill in *A Clergyman's Daughter.*

Unlike *Burmese Days,* which presents its developing story in a conventional sequence of short chapters, *A Clergyman's Daughter* employs five long "chapters" (really sections) that are further subdivided. This arrangement recurs alternately through Orwell's fiction, *Coming Up for Air* being in five long "parts," *Nineteen Eighty-Four* in three. Its use is not random: these three novels have in common that their emphasis is not so much on story, and even less on plot, as on the exposure of their main characters to varieties and levels of experience different from those in which they find themselves at the beginning. George Bowling thinks back to his rural birthplace, then tries to go back there; these excursions in time and space only prove that, in Thomas Wolfe's phrase, "you can't go home again," and at the end Bowling is back where he started, in the uncongenial modern world, Winston Smith finds a temporary refuge from totalitarianism in his affair with Julia, only to fall into the hands of the Thought Police and end up deprived even of the wish to rebel against Big Brother. In *A Clergyman's Daughter* Dorothy Hare returns after the experience of hop-picking, destitution, and teaching to her dreary round and common tasks in Knype Hill. The novel's circular shape embodies the ineluctability of Dorothy's situation, one which its generic title suggests Orwell saw as typical of a whole class of spinsterish Christian Marthas.

The novel's first section, its longest, describes a single day in Dorothy's hard-working life as the not very pretty only daughter of the rector of St. Athelstan's, Charles Hare, who has alienated two-thirds of his congregation by a mixture of personal chilliness and an old-fashioned High Anglican form of service displeasing to the Evangelical and Anglo-Catholic wings of the parish alike. Though he is punctilious about his strictly religious duties ("If it had been urgently necessary he would have walked twenty miles through snow to baptize a dying baby"[268]), his disdain for a clergyman's more mundane jobs, like church organizations and parish visiting, has made him unpopular;

public-school educated, the cousin of a baronet, he would have been more at home, Orwell states, "a couple of centuries earlier" as "a happy pluralist." L. P. Hartley called him "a monster",[14] but he was wrong. Not only is Orwell's description of him virtually identical with two lines in a poem he wrote about himself in 1935 ("A happy vicar I might have been / Two hundred years ago";[15] both his name and his circumstances originate from Orwell's own family. His paternal grandfather, Thomas Blair, was the poor cousin of an earl, married a girl called Fanny Hare, and spent his last thirteen years as a country vicar. Orwell could easily have chosen his descriptive details differently if he had wanted to distance himself from Dorothy and her father.

Dorothy's day is a busy one, made more so by her father's detachment. It is she who must fend off the tradesmen's bills, since she cannot persuade him to pay them by selling some of his shares in losing concerns; she who must worry about the ruinous fabric of the church building; she who must listen to the vain appeals of the church school headmaster for more ritual in the services; she who must run the Girl Guides, rub embrocation on a devout parishioner's tired rheumatic legs, and spend hours, as Orwell had done at the Hawthorns, constructing costumes for the school pageant out of brown paper and glue. She must also dodge the prurient stories of Mrs. Semprill, the malignant local gossip, while taking care not to give rise to more of them by succumbing to the casual but persistent advances of Mr. Warburton, a freethinking painter with three illegitimate children who recalls Aldous Huxley's John Bidlake in *Point Counter Point* (1928). Here, however, she is in no danger; as if further to box her into her fate, Orwell gives her a loathing of any sexual contact, "the special incurable disability that she carried through life" (301).

What sustains her is a mixture of self-discipline and faith. The latter expresses itself both negatively and positively. Catching herself in any un-Christian, sacrilegious, uncharitable thought, like her fear that, at communion, she will have to take the chalice after the old, decrepit, slobbery Miss Mayfill,[16] she sticks a pin into her arm. But inhaling the rich summer scents of trees and flowers as she rides her bicycle home, she feels intensely—before worrying that she is merely indulging in "nature-worship"—"that mystical joy in the beauty of the earth and the very nature of things that she recognized, perhaps mistakenly, as the love of God" (287). The details of her conscientious life, spent in an atmosphere of decaying, genteel penury, are conveyed with what can be called, equally, vividness and grinding realism: one pities and admires Dorothy at once.

Orwell removes her from Knype Hill with incredible abruptness in chapter 2. Her evening has been spent at the house of Mr. Warburton, whom she likes in spite of his incorrigible advances and his impiety; indeed, "she got from him . . . a species of sympathy and understanding which she could not get elsewhere" (279). It is that convenient fictional stereotype, the attraction of opposites. After arguments about faith and the usual resisted passes, Dorothy has been unable to avoid a good-night kiss at the gate, which she fears Mrs. Semprill may have seen (Orwell inflates this unimportant detail later into a mechanism to delay Dorothy's return home). Back at the rectory, she resumes the making of jackboots for the pageant, waiting for the hard glue to melt. As if immediately after, the reader next encounters her waking to "a species of consciousness," having lost her memory and with no idea who she is, in a shabby south London street. For form's sake, as her subsequent adventures are intended as realism, not as dream vision, Orwell sketches in a few perfunctory "explanations," but essentially her amnesia is no more than a device to catapult her passively into new experience. In Aristotelian terms it is possible rather than artistically probable, and three years later Orwell was willing to admit as much. In *Coming Up for Air,* George Bowling is faced with the need to explain to his wife his absence in Lower Binfield: he refuses "to pull the old gag about losing my memory."[17]

Having no reason to do otherwise, and anyway having no money, Dorothy joins up with a small group of down-and-outs who hope to get work in the Kentish hop fields. The whole of chapter 2 is hardly more than a repetition, often verbatim and exact almost to the day, of Orwell's own experiences in the late summer of 1931, which he wrote up that October in an unpublished essay called "Hop-Picking." The young man who befriends Dorothy, the red-haired Nobby, is not modeled on but identical with the "Ginger" whom Orwell met, an habitual thief who would, in both texts, "steal anything that was not tied down." The hop-pickers' songs, which Orwell preserved in 1931, surface unaltered in 1934, and many of Orwell's descriptive details and comments, on, for instance, the economics of hop-picking and the food eaten by hop-pickers, have an interest that is sociological, in the manner of *Down and Out in Paris and London,* rather than fictional. The comments are not Dorothy's, and Orwell does not seem to want to show her as learning anything from her experiences, except insofar as they offer a kind of undifferentiated proletarian warmth, and a sense of "physical joy" that is the result of tiredness and hard work. "The sun burned down upon you, baking you brown, and the bitter, never-palling scent, like a wind from oceans of cool beer, flowed into your nostrils and refreshed you" (321). Even here, the lyricism of "oceans of cool beer" is surely Orwellian rather than characteristic of Dorothy.

The eventual arrest of Nobby for stealing from local farms disturbs Dorothy's passivity, precipitating the sudden recognition that it is her photograph in a recent copy of *Pippin's Weekly,* she who is the "Rector's Daughter" of newspaper headlines, vanished from home and presumed, as a result of Mrs. Semprill's gossip, to be somewhere on the continent with Mr. Warburton, who is there, quite innocently, with his three children. Writing to her father for money, and getting no reply, she concludes that he believes the Semprill version, and feels unable to go home because of the scandal. At the same time, hearing church bells and feeling homesick, she realizes that she has lost her faith: "she was aware that she had no longer the smallest impulse to pray. . . . Prayer had no meaning for her any longer" (335). But there is no evidence to suggest that her life in the hop fields, per se, has had anything to do with this; the author shirks his job, and the reader is left to surmise that Orwell thought faith a habit and state of mind, which an abrupt change in one's circumstances could easily erase.[18]

The novel's central and shortest section (chap. 3), set in Trafalgar Square, is the nadir of Dorothy's experience: a cold late autumn night, followed by two more like it, among London's down-and-outs, including some of her companions from Kent, but also an unfrocked clergyman, Mr. Tallboys, and a woman turned out of doors by her husband—an extension, perhaps, of Mrs. Morel in D. H. Lawrence's *Sons and Lovers.* Unable, after the end of the hop-picking season in September, to obtain work as a domestic servant—her educated accent and ragged clothes are alike against her—Dorothy is reduced to sleeping in the open and begging. Again Orwell is making use of his own experience, but this time more imaginatively. This section of the novel was in fact the only one he ever professed himself "pleased with," in a letter to Brenda Salkeld shortly before publication.[19] He had read James Joyce's *Ulysses* with great admiration at the end of 1932, and emulated its long "Nighttown" section, which concludes part 2, by casting the first section of chapter 3 into a quasi-dramatic form: more exactly, into a sequence of short, sometimes recurring utterances that are partly dialogue and partly "choral" outbursts, interspersed with "stage directions" confined mostly to dispassionate description, an unwonted act of self-discipline on Orwell's part.

V. S. Pritchett's view was that this "'stunt' Joyce fashion utterly ruins the effect";[20] certainly the Joycean panache of Mr. Tallboys's fin-de-siècle mode of speech is out of keeping with the ordinary language, wry, despairing, forcedly cheerful, of the other down-and-outs. The real problem with Orwell's chosen method is that, though it allows him to display much in a comparatively short space, and does not lack power in the vision of essentially separate predicaments joined by "the horrible communism of the Square" (361), it does not allow Dorothy herself more than a fragmentary role. As with the hop-picking section, the reader can only infer Dorothy's reaction to what goes on around her. Its actual expression is restricted to a single remark, horrified and compassionate, but never to blossom later in action or reflection: "Oh how can you all stand it? Surely you don't have to do this every night of your lives?"(354).

Dorothy herself does not. Her eventual arrest, and brief detention, for begging coincides with her father's successful efforts to trace her, which he does through his cousin the baronet, an elderly man who looks like "a well-meaning but exceptionally brainless prawn" (364), and whose affinity with characters in P. G. Wodehouse extends to his having a capable butler who resembles Bertie Wooster's Jeeves. Because of the "scandal," there is as yet no prospect of Dorothy's returning home; she is given a modest sum of money and found a job at a small private school in "Southbridge,"[21] "a repellent suburb ten or a dozen miles from London." The school, owned by Mrs. Creevy, Dickensian in name, and of a Dickensian meanness and malignity—unlike the rector she really is a monster—is of an abysmally low standard, existing mostly to profit financially from lower-middle-class snobbery. Dorothy is the sole teacher and finds in her classroom no maps, no pictures, no books, no geometrical instruments, and pupils who know nothing but neat handwriting and practical arithmetic. Dorothy "had not known that schools of this description still existed in the civilized world" (376). Gerald Gould, who assessed Orwell's manuscript for Gollancz, also found it incredible, but his reaction was greeted by Orwell with sardonic amusement.

The depressing situation presented in chapter 4 brings out the best in Dorothy, who is, at the school, closest to her previous experience in Knype Hill. Ill-paid and ill-fed, she nevertheless devotes herself to "rescuing these children from the horrible darkness in which they had been kept" (377). She brings books, introduces the students to Shakespeare, gets them to make a contour map of Europe: "their warped little minds seemed to spring up and expand like daisies when you move the garden roller off them" (381). Orwell's own concern with education makes itself very much felt here: unlike that of Ursula Brangwen in D. H. Lawrence's *The Rainbow,* whose classroom is a place where the teacher struggles to dominate and control, Dorothy's effort is to impart knowledge, and the brief period during which she contrives to do so would offer a useful vademecum to anyone in her situation. The interest of the section is indeed documentary rather than strictly fictional. In many places, Orwell makes not the slightest attempt to subsume general authorial comment into his character's responses.[22]

Dorothy's experiments are short-lived. Parental complaints ("We don't send our children to school to have ideas put into their heads" [388]) soon return her to Mrs. Creevy's view of her proper place, as a drudge who must learn "the dismal arts of the school-teacher" (404). She sinks further and further into discipline problems with the disappointed pupils, the dullness of rote learning, melancholy, and loneliness.

The final chapter of the book, however, brings Dorothy rescue, just as she has suddenly been dismissed at the end of the Easter term. She is rescued physically by Mr. Warburton, who arrives in a taxi as she is leaving the school, and in story terms by the fact that the "scandal" is now over. Mrs. Semprill has been discredited and Dorothy can return to a father less captious than before, and of whom she is fond. The train journey home is spent partly in a discussion of Dorothy's lost faith, which means nothing to Warburton, and in Dorothy's rejection of his offer of marriage, backed up though that is by an only too credible prediction of her future in the parish, a future likely to worsen after her father dies. Such thoughts, and "more outward things like poverty and drudgery," are less worrying to Dorothy than "the deadly emptiness she had discovered at the heart of things" (422). She retains a "mind naturally pious," and has been comforted at Southbridge by a sense that, even without religious belief, church services represent "something of dignity, of spiritual comeliness" (398), a view the traditionalist in Orwell probably never lost. Nevertheless there remains for her the inescapable theoretical dilemma: "Either life on earth is a preparation for something greater and more lasting, or it is meaningless, dark and dreadful" (423). What counters this for Dorothy is the equally inescapable daily round to which she has chosen—and for once it is a choice—to return: the putting in order of parish affairs, which her father had let slide, and the preparations for yet another fund-raising pageant. The novel ends with her making costumes as before, "in the penetrating smell of the glue-pot," and with Orwell's own gloss on her new life, whose raison d'être she is not yet conscious of but can "only live"; "if one gets on with the job that lies to hand the ultimate purpose of the job fades into insignificance; . . . faith and no faith are very much the same provided that one is doing what is customary, useful and acceptable" (424–25). This, and it is surely Orwell's own attitude to life, is hardly intellectually profound; yet it provokes the reader's admiration. It is not clear, however, that the loss of religious faith that gives rise to it is convincingly located in Dorothy's outward experiences as recounted by the novel. She herself discards them, feeling that it is "only the things that happen in your heart that matter" (422).[23] By having her do so, Orwell comes dangerously close to reducing three-fifths of the novel to a species of conjuring trick that distracts the reader from her inward change, rather than illuminates it. Dorothy's faith is a matter of "now you see it, now you don't."

In fact, the dominant idea left by the novel is not of faith or loss of faith but of resilience, and it gives a powerful portrayal of this, despite its faults as a piece of fiction. The resilience shown is specifically that of a duty-minded upper-middle-class person, like Orwell himself, and to that extent Orwell and Dorothy are one. Dorothy, however, is a female protagonist and Orwell, whose ideas about women were conventional and unthoughtful, makes her resilience take the form of a passive acceptance that his male protagonists do not show. She is consigned to Knype Hill to find or make her life, and here she and Orwell diverge. It was to be a while longer before he discovered his own authentic area of effort. Together with *Burmese Days, A Clergyman's Daughter* encapsulates large tracts of Orwell's earlier experience, and so allows him to discard them. Having done so, and within a month of sending the novel to his agent, Orwell left Southwold.

Keep the Aspidistra Flying (1936)

Orwell's third novel carries over both its title phrase and its epigraph from its immediate predecessor. The aspidistra seems to have been something of an obsession with Orwell in the 1930s, perhaps not surprisingly: its gloomy dark green leaves once adorned so many English homes that it gave rise to one of the most mournfully ear-splitting songs of Gracie Fields, the popular singer from northern England whose heyday was the interwar years, "It's the biggest aspidistra in the world."[24] Orwell mentions the plant in his first two novels, and in *A Clergyman's Daughter* the unfrocked clergyman Mr. Tallboys also sets it to music, singing the exhortation "Keep the aspidistra flying" to the tune of "Deutschland, Deutschland über alles" in Trafalgar Square (349). The title of Orwell's third novel has thus the not altogether ironic ring of a national anthem.

The epigraph is first referred to a little later in *A Clergyman's Daughter,* near the beginning of chapter 4. Thinking about the contrast between the "miserable struggle of three weeks ago" and "the ease with which this job at Mrs. Creevy's school had been found for her," Dorothy Hare calls to mind "a favourite saying of Mr. Warburton's," to the effect that "if you took I Corinthians, chapter thirteen, and in every verse wrote 'money' instead of 'charity', the chapter had ten times as much meaning as before" (367). At the beginning of *Keep the Aspidistra Flying,* Orwell quotes the relevant verses of 1 Corinthians, chapter 13, in precisely this way, presenting money as the modern all-encompassing replacement for the supreme Christian virtue. Before interpreting the novel, however, as a simplistic, whether cynical or scathing, vision of the power of money, the reader needs to take account of two matters. Though a useful foil to Dorothy, Mr. Warburton is by no means the mouthpiece of Orwell himself in *A Clergyman's Daughter*; and even if he were, to give more than a casual glance at the altered Bible quotation is to realize that it says a number of good things about money. If the evidence of the novel shows that both the absence and the presence of money can have unfortunate effects, it also demonstrates that money is far from being the root of all evil, but can make possible something of that "comeliness" of life that in *A Clergyman's Daughter* is brought by religious observances. As the title of *Keep the Aspidistra Flying* is not wholly debunking, so its epigraph, and its contents, are not wholly negative.

Orwell began working on his third novel a few months after leaving Southwold in November 1934 and coming to the "literary" London suburb of Hampstead, where he divided his day between writing and acting as a part-time assistant in "Booklovers' Corner," a bookshop owned by friends of his aunt Nellie Limouzin, who was involved with the Independent Labour Party. He first mentioned the novel in a letter to Brenda Salkeld in February 1935, saying that he wanted "this one to be a work of art"—by contrast, presumably, with *A Clergyman's Daughter.*[25] Quite what Orwell meant by such a term is hard to say; perhaps only that he was concerned with its "external style," since a letter to Rayner Heppenstall in September speaks of his having "three more chapters and an epilogue to do," after which he would spend "about two months putting on the twiddly bits."[26] Such a revealing admission to a fellow writer suggests a superficial view of "art," one little bothered by the sense of inevitability that a work of fiction needs to possess in order to convince. It is certainly true that, in *Keep the Aspidistra Flying,* Orwell allowed only the minimum of "assimilation time" to elapse between his new Hampstead circumstances and the fictional use he made of them; in this respect his third novel is much more "raw" than its predecessors.

But though it may seem too hasty and opportunistic for a young writer of thirty-one, currently working in a Hampstead bookshop, to make his protagonist a writer of twenty-nine also working in a Hampstead bookshop, the novel's irritation with a society predicated on money is more deeply rooted in Orwell's experience, and its protagonist's struggle to fulfill himself in such a society is a predicament Orwell had been familiar with for some years. This element gives *Keep the Aspidistra Flying* some strength of feeling, which reviewers recognized when it appeared in April 1936, four months after completion, though it sold fewer copies (twenty-five hundred) than its predecessor, and ten years later Orwell linked it with *A Clergyman's Daughter* as a book he was "ashamed of" and had only written because he was "desperate for money."[27] That reason, if true, is wholly appropriate to the world the novel depicts, and one its protagonist would have understood, though his story makes it clear that, unlike the Orwell he partly resembles, he would have lacked the drive to produce a substantial work.

It would require too much space to indicate the precise extent to which the protagonist, Gordon Comstock, both is and is not Orwell; but the matter must be touched on since it partly determines one's view of Orwell's intentions in the novel, that is, of how far Comstock's attitudes and behavior are meant to elicit sympathy and how far disapproval. Louis Simpson, reviewing the novel when it finally appeared in the United States in 1956, stated that Comstock was "an Orwell without Orwell's talent," a temptingly neat but inaccurate formula.[28] There are senses, in fact, in which it is true to say that Comstock has Orwell's talent and more. Though by the end of 1934, the point at which the novel begins, Comstock has published only one book, whereas Orwell had published two and completed a third, that one book is described as appearing when Comstock was twenty-seven, an age at which Orwell had hardly started work on *Down and Out in Paris and London.* That Comstock is a poet, author of the "exceptionally promising" slim volume *Mice,* does not serve to differentiate the nature of his talent from Orwell's. Orwell was still writing and publishing poems in 1934, and the very poem Comstock slowly assembles over the first seven chapters of *Keep the Aspidistra Flying* appeared with little alteration over Orwell's name in the November 1935 issue of the *Adelphi,* entitled "St. Andrew's Day, 1935." "Ravelston would print it," thinks Comstock in chapter 4; Sir Richard Rees did, as he had also printed in the *Adelphi* of April 1934 a poem of Orwell's employing to similar effect the "Buridan's donkey" image that occurs in chapter 5 in a conversation between Comstock and Ravelston.[29] Just as, toward the end of the novel, Comstock throws away the incomplete manuscript of "London Pleasures," with its archaic rhyme royal stanzas, so Orwell failed to finish the epic poem he was writing at the same period, a history of England from the time of Chaucer.

The link created by these similarities of artistic career is strengthened by Orwell's placing Comstock (as Dorothy Hare earlier) in situations he himself had experienced. Gordon's excursion with his girlfriend Rosemary Waterlow to Burnham Beeches, a beauty spot west of London (chap. 7) recapitulates Orwell's own visit there a year earlier with Eleanor Jaques, even to making use of the excruciatingly embarrassing lunch at a pretentious hotel;[30] and, like Comstock in chapter 8, Orwell had entertained a number of friends in an expensive London restaurant and proceeded to get drunk.[31] Many of the details in chapter 9, when Comstock wakes up to find himself in a police cell, are directly transcribed from Orwell's essay "Clink," written in August 1932 to record the success of his attempt the previous Christmas to get arrested for being drunk and disorderly. Biographical evidence also indicates the close similarity between many of Comstock's opinions and prejudices and those of Orwell, from his distrust of "success" to his view that "a man pays for a woman, a woman doesn't pay for a man" (651).

Similarity is not identity, however. Orwell's essay "Bookshop Memories," published in November 1936,[32] makes it clear that his experiences in the Hampstead bookshop did not inspire quite the seething irritation and "inert hatred" felt by Comstock, and the biographical record attests to the fact that his Hampstead period was far more pleasant, and far more social, than that of his character. The control and distancing exerted by the effort to redeploy aspects of oneself in a work of fiction, and by the deliberate recollection of experiences already left behind, is itself a factor to be recognized. A more accurate version of the Louis Simpson formula would be that, for much of the novel, Comstock is an Orwell without Orwell's stamina, perseverance, and balance. The first ten chapters represent the author reliving earlier phases of himself in a concentrated and extreme form, and using fiction as a mechanism for release, self-criticism, and eventual purgation. But the point, in spring 1935, when Comstock escapes from what is essentially a neurotic state of hostility and alienation is also the point at which he abandons his long poem and with it his ambitions to be a creative writer. Whatever negative elements in himself Orwell had needed to overcome, he had not himself found it impossible to continue to write.

A final hint of how Orwell viewed Comstock in relation to himself may be offered by the very name he gave him. He calls Gordon Comstock, at the start of chapter 3, "a pretty bloody name," but only actually comments on the "Gordon" part of it, an aspect of "the Scotchification of England" (598) that he disliked at this time and that may have contributed to his name change from "Eric Blair." He says nothing about "Comstock," a far from common surname. He had read the works of George Bernard Shaw at Eton, and in 1905 Shaw coined the term "Comstockery," after one Anthony Comstock (1844–1915), who founded the Society for the Suppression of Vice. The term passed into American (though not British) usage, with the meaning "immoderate censorship on grounds of immorality."[33] Orwell's Comstock, though indifferent to "vice" in the Victorian sense, is characterized by immoderate feelings, whether in his hostility to much in society, his final rejection of his own poetry, or his zealous convert's insistence, even though it involves a quarrel with Rosemary, on buying an aspidistra for their newlyweds' living room. It is tempting to think that Orwell's choice of name for his main character both labeled an aspect of himself and set himself apart from it.

The novel has an outward appearance of symmetry, most of its twelve chapters being of roughly the same length; but its treatment of time and event is in fact lopsided. It is less concerned to tell an evenly developing story than to present a predicament, in a series of tableaux occupying the first nine chapters and covering a period of only two weeks in considerable detail. The tenth chapter, encapsulating some three months, presents Comstock at the lowest and extremest point of his alienation from society, a state from which he emerges not as the result of any inward illumination but because of an external demand, which he is too decent to deny, the pregnancy of his girl. The last two chapters, together covering two more months but actually describing two widely separated days, introduce this spur to action and, briefly, Comstock's resumption, because of it, of a way of life that at the start of the novel he has deliberately abandoned. Different critics have seen this resumption of "normality" variously, as a triumph and as a defeat. It is, in fact, difficult to see it as either of these. Any sense of it as a defeat is effectively undercut by the pointlessly negative quality of most of Comstock's previous experience: he seems to have little to lose. Conversely, any view of the ending as a victory, even only for common sense, involves, on one level, being able to set aside the cliché of plot that brings it about, and on another more important level, being able to consider as mere froth, or as a delaying tactic, the dissatisfaction with bourgeois society that has been preached through most of the novel.

The first two chapters, set in the bookshop where Comstock works for two pounds a week, and then in the "dingy and depressing" lodgings that cost him nearly two-thirds of his meager wage, plunge the reader into Comstock's dissatisfaction with such intensity that it is neither easy to stand back from it nor, apparently, intended that one should. One sympathizes quickly with a poor man who has only a few pence to last him until payday, and with a struggling writer oppressed by the weight of other people's books and envious of the success enjoyed by "those moneyed young beasts who glide so gracefully from Eton to Cambridge, and from Cambridge to the literary reviews" (580). It is also possible to admire someone who, though desperate for a drink at his local pub, rejects this option because it would involve sponging on an acquaintance: "You can't let other people buy your drinks for you" (592). All around him Comstock smells the "money-stink" of a world that excludes him, sapping his will to write and souring his friendships with the embarrassments and subterfuges of financial inequality. The poem (Orwell's own) that Comstock slowly begins to frame in chapter 1 as a comment on the "menacing wind" of late November has, by the time of its completion in chapter 7, become a vision of a whole society ruled by "the money-god," in which wage-earners are terrified of losing their jobs, harassed by bills, and forced into contraception because of the cost of children.

By this point, however, the reader's perspective on Comstock's situation has widened, making sympathy not so easy, though not impossible, to extend. Chapter 3 fills the interval between one day and the next with a flashback of Comstock's history, as a member of the "landless gentry" and the last male scion of a once prosperous Victorian family in which, now, "nothing ever happens." Educated, to the impoverishment of his parents' remaining finances and his sister's future, at a school where, as at St. Cyprian's, all the boys were "richer than he was," Comstock has emerged from "a crawling reverence for money" into a realization that there are only two genuine possibilities in life: "You can possess money or you can despise money and fail to get it" (603).

Certainly Comstock does not worship money; but he can neither possess it nor despise it. His first dull job bores him, but abandoning it at twenty-four in order to write only exposes him to the rigors of near starvation and the guilty humiliation of sponging off Julia, his sister who works in a tea shop. When he at last finds a job in an advertising agency, the New Albion, and seems because of a flair for copywriting in danger of succeeding in "the dirtiest ramp that capitalism has yet produced" (608), he determines to get out while there is still time into something that will keep body and soul together but not compromise his declaration, made in adolescence, of war against money. What seems exactly to fit the bill is the "blind-alley job" at the bookshop, where he has been for two years when the book opens. Nevertheless, if Comstock himself has come to feel that "failure is as great a swindle as success," the reader can hardly now ignore one simple fact not available at the beginning. Comstock's unfortunate circumstances—an almost halved salary does not keep body and soul together—are at least partly a self-inflicted wound.

Aware of this, the reader may still respect Comstock's principles, his refusal to become a beneficiary of the commercial world he despises. Inherent in this respect, however, is likely to be the expectation that, having made his bed, he can lie on it without complaint; and even that he should possess some nobility or stoicism that will give weight to his poor opinion of the world. The next three chapters frustrate such expectations by showing Comstock's personality in relation to particular events and people. His disappointment when he finds the reviewer and critic Paul Doring, "a very mangy lion," not at home (chap. 4) is understandable, as is his long tramp through the lights of central London feeling penniless and excluded; but his sense of a deliberate snub is inaccurate and egocentric, and when in chapter 5 he refuses a further invitation, the inexcusable rudeness of his letter outweighs anything admirable in its romantically self-destructive gesture. Nor can one find anything but self-pity and willingness to wound another when he responds to a rejection slip from the "snooty" "Primrose Quarterly" by sending an anonymous note to Rosemary bearing only the melodramatic phrase "You have broken my heart" (625).

Chapters 5 and 6 introduce the two people closest to Comstock, both of whom are portrayed with palpable affection and thus not only cause the reader to view the main character from a greater distance, but suggest that this effect was intended by Orwell. Despite the enormous difference in their incomes, Comstock "adores" Ravelston: not because, as editor of the socialist monthly *Antichrist,* he publishes Comstock's poems but because he possesses "a kind of fundamental decency, a graceful attitude to life," which is a function of his wealth. What emerges from their long conversation, concerned partly with the difficulties of courting when you have no money, is that although Comstock feels acutely "the futility, the bloodiness, the deathliness of modern life" (629), he does not share Ravelston's hopeful socialism. Political theories are beyond the reach of one afflicted with the "spiritual halitosis" of poverty: "Give me five quid a week and I'd be a Socialist," he admits to Ravelston, whose socialism is even more paradoxically coexistent with wealth, though not less genuine for that.

But where respect, and self-respect, understandably operate to make him refuse the loan pressed on him by Ravelston, Comstock frequently borrows from his impecunious sister, since families "don't count" (655). And when he refuses in chapter 6 to let Rosemary buy him a meal, his independence seems merely perverse, to the reader and to her, especially as it is accompanied by one of the many beliefs that Comstock delights in clinging to, that it is women who are obsessed by money, wanting it for "a house of her own and two babies and Drage furniture and an aspidistra" (635). Where Comstock worries at his prejudices like a dog with a bone, Rosemary has only tolerance for an alienation she cannot understand. Where Comstock sees his sexual frustration in terms of a logical bind: "Serve the money-god or do without women—those are the only alternatives. And both were equally impossible" (643); Rosemary has the ordinary human doubts of a woman who, though in love, is hesitant about physical lovemaking and sees no possibility of marriage on two pounds a week.[35] Orwell renders the tensions of their relationship with an alert sensitivity, balancing the ranting Lawrentian generalizations that open chapter 6 ("This woman business! What a bore it is! What a pity we can't cut it right out, or at least be like the animals—minutes of ferocious lust and months of icy chastity") with a phrase whose sanity and lyricism offers promise for the lovers' future: "Each was to the other a standing joke and an object infinitely precious" (650).

Their excursion to Burnham Beeches in chapter 7, the longest chapter in the novel, opens with a single sentence paragraph that is clearly one of Orwell's "twiddly-bits." "The plumes of the chimneys floated perpendicular against skies of smoky rose." The idyllic expectation set up by this is confirmed by a morning of walking during which Comstock and Rosemary are "extravagantly happy"; like characters in a fairy story, they respond to the freakishly perfect weather and the beauty of the countryside with "a sort of sexless rapture, like children." The afternoon brings reality, however. The only lunch they can find is in a disastrously expensive hotel with a supercilious waiter, and the lovemaking to which Comstock has been looking forward—Orwell reproduces its awkward, willed, embarrassed quality with flesh-creeping accuracy—is frustrated first by Rosemary's fear of pregnancy and later by Comstock's inability to forget the pressing financial problem of the fare home.

The episode reveals Comstock's unpleasantness in inflicting his various problems on Rosemary: money, sex, and the will to power seem inextricably linked. But if this chapter shows the unpleasant effects of money's absence, the one that follows seems deliberately juxtaposed in order to show how its presence can be equally harmful. Unexpectedly receiving fifty dollars (then worth about ten pounds) for a poem accepted in an American magazine, and not unreasonably wanting to celebrate, Comstock goes much too far: the vulgarity of his display is no better than the bourgeois scruples he exhibits when he is poor. For all his repeated protestations, his sister, to whom half the money should rightly go, is forgotten, and despite a momentary chill of consciousness of "awful folly" (681), he follows up the pointless extravagance of his entertainment of Rosemary and Ravelston with a crude sexual pass at the former that provokes the latter's rare indignation, and then by dragging the embarrassed Ravelston into a drunken entanglement with two prostitutes. His later self-loathing reflection that "if you have no money you don't even know how to spend it when you get it" (chap. 9) may proceed from Orwell's wish to disarm criticism of Comstock's behavior but cannot mitigate the reader's sense that Comstock's earlier tirades against the money world have no true intellectual basis.

The practical effect of his immoderate behavior is first to get him arrested for assaulting a policeman, then to lose him his job when his employer reads a stray newspaper report. The force majeure of circumstances at last obliges him to accept help and hospitality from Ravelston; but when Rosemary asks him to return to his original job at the New Albion, where she, incidentally, has been quietly working all the time without being presented as a lackey or dupe of capitalism, he refuses, saying: "I'd sooner sink than rise" (chap. 9). Chapter 10 shows him doing this, in a job in a cheap lending library in the poor district of Lambeth. Ironically, though less well paid than in Hampstead, he is better off, but only because he has no appearances to keep up. His squalid room is "suited to my situation," he tells a pained, uncomprehending Ravelston; he is "under ground," anonymous, sunk in a drop-out apathy he enjoys: "Without regret, almost intentionally, he was letting himself go to pieces" (711). Gradually, over the winter months, he recedes from family, friends, and respectability.

He cannot, however, recede from Rosemary, who out of "magnanimity, pure magnanimity" comes to his room and, in a reversal of the Burnham Beeches episode, insists on making love. The fictional, if not necessarily realistic, predictability of the outcome allows Orwell to move his character out of an impasse that has no glimmer of the heroic about it, and show him, in the last two chapters, shouldering the responsibilities of fatherhood: though, in doing so, he makes a gesture in the direction of the "theme" of the larger part of the book: "It is when [the money god] gets at you through your sense of decency that he finds you helpless" (726). Yet although Orwell allows Comstock some face-saving exclamations about the advertising world of Bovex, Vitamalt, and bathroom tissue that now seems his unavoidable destiny, one does not feel that any great sacrifice of principle is being made.[36] The prospect of a child, flesh of his flesh, shifts the novel's focus. Comstock is driven back to "decent fully human life" of which money seems, now, an integral part, by "some force outside himself," and his analysis of his feelings at "chucking up the sponge" leads to a conclusion likely to be shared by the reader: "There was a peculiar sensation, an actual physical sensation in his heart, in his limbs, all over him. What was it? Shame, misery, despair? Rage at being back in the clutch of money? Boredom when he thought of the deadly future? He dragged the sensation forth, faced it, examined it. It was relief" (730).

Like Flory in *Burmese Days,* Comstock has been operating "outside the stream of life." Unlike Flory, he is able to become part of it, thanks to what one can hardly avoid calling "the love of a good woman"—a woman, in fact, almost too good to be true. The last chapter, whose banality has only the faintest traces of the sardonic, shows him earning his respectable four pounds, ten shillings a week, and absorbed in a deodorant advertising campaign, the domesticities of furnishing an apartment, and the prospect that "once again things were happening in the Comstock family." If hardly a victory, the ending represents the average human compromise in an imperfect world, one that Comstock has taken longer than most to reach.

Some of the buoyancy of the conclusion must be attributed to Orwell's circumstances at the time. In spring 1935 he had met Eileen O'Shaughnessy (aged thirty, like Rosemary), an Oxford English graduate pursuing a course in psychology at London University. Five months after the novel was finished, they married. It would therefore be flying in the face of external fact to see Comstock's marriage as a defeat; though in giving him an office job and treating that job as incompatible with writing, Orwell differentiates Comstock from himself. *Keep the Aspidistra Flying* is not, however, any more satisfactory as a novel because its ending reflects its author's new happiness. In fictional terms, its outcome is contrived, and Orwell may have realized this when, in chapter 11, he describes Comstock's position between "outsider" detachment and married responsibility as "a pretty banal predicament." And if the ending is predictably sane and ordinary, how is one to take most of the novel's opposition of the evils of a money society and the ills of a life without money except as shadowboxing with vituperative accompaniment? Part of the novel's unsatisfactoriness may proceed from something ignoble inherent in its material. Certainly Cyril Connolly felt this, saying in 1936 that "the obsession with money about which the book is written, is one which must prevent it from achieving the proportions of a work of art."[37] But it was Dorothy van Ghent, reviewing it on its appearance in America in 1936, who brilliantly identified its crucial shortcoming, one related to its total aim and to the jarring elements that compose it: "One does not really know what the book is about . . . the problem of maintaining normal identity in the lower-middle-class is broken in two like a surrealist cadaver with the legs of Don Quixote and the face of Dagwood, smiling from ear to ear."[38]

Coming Up for Air (1939)

For two years after *Keep the Aspidistra Flying* was finished, in January 1936, Orwell was occupied with two entirely new experiences, among the unemployed and the miners in northern England, and with the Republican forces in the Spanish Civil War. He was occupied too with the writing up of those experiences in *The Road to Wigan Pier* (1937) and *Homage to Catalonia* (1938). These two works of nonfiction will be treated in the next chapter, since they mark a decisive shift in Orwell's development, which from 1936 was characterized by the large increase in political awareness noted by Orwell himself in "Why I Write" (1946), and by a predilection for various sorts of journalism rather than for novels. They presage the great period of Orwell's political, cultural, and literary essays, which runs from 1939 to 1948. This period also includes *Animal Farm* and *Nineteen Eighty-Four*; but these, though cast in fictional form, are differentiated by their strong political intention from Orwell's prewar novels. Though *Coming Up For Air* is technically Orwell's fourth novel, in a real sense it can also be regarded as his last one; and, in that it not only looks around at contemporary England under the shadow of approaching war, but also gathers up Orwell's earliest English experiences in one comprehensive and final backward glance, it is appropriate to deal with it in this chapter, despite the leapfrog involved over the two nonfictional works that precede it.

Orwell first mentioned the possibility of "my next novel" in a letter to the writer Jack Common in 1938, shortly after he had completed *Homage to Catalonia*.[39] The imaginative trigger of *Coming Up for Air,* which juxtaposes the present threat of the "bombing plane" with the peaceful landscapes before the Great War, may perhaps have been Orwell's first sight of southern England when he returned from Spain in June 1937, the description of which he used to conclude his book about his Spanish experiences: "Down here it was still the England I had known in my childhood: the railway cuttings smothered in wild flowers, the deep meadows where the great shining horses browse and meditate, the slow-moving streams bordered by willows, the green bosoms of the elms, the lark-spurs in the cottage gardens . . . all sleeping the deep, deep sleep of England, from which I sometimes fear that we shall never wake until we are jerked out of it by the roar of bombs."

It is a beautiful passage; but it is entirely characteristic of the new, politically conscious Orwell that he should move from appreciation in the present not only to fear of the future, but to registering, along with that fear, a sense that such soporific beauty needed to be awakened from, as if the ascetic in him were fighting the aesthete. In *Keep the Aspidistra Flying,* the thought of future bombs acts as a boredom-reliever, safety valve, and vicarious avenger for the alienated Gordon Comstock. Here no such nihilism is apparent, perhaps because by late 1937 (with Guernica in April) the bombs had come to seem inevitable. In *Coming Up for Air* one actually drops, though only by accident; and what the novel sets against this new, inescapable reality is the sense that beautiful landscapes, and the innocence they represent, are a thing of the past.

Two elements only incidental in *Keep the Aspidistra Flying* find their fruition in *Coming Up for Air.* Toward the end of the novel, having made his decision to marry Rosemary and, in consequence, return to the advertising agency, Gordon Comstock walks through a respectable lower-middle-class area. An unaccustomed mellowness causes him to wonder "about the people in houses like those," who include "shop-assistants, commercial travellers, insurance touts" (732). George Bowling, the insurance salesman protagonist of *Coming Up for Air,* is an only slightly more prosperous example of such people, and his character is partly anticipated in Comstock's fellow lodger in Hampstead, the beer-drinking and barmaid-chasing Flaxman, who is temporarily separated from his wife. If the hero of *Keep the Aspidistra Flying* is a distorted but recognizable version of the idealistic Don Quixote, the main character of *Coming Up for Air* is an antihero, a kind of Sancho Panza; though George Bowling is sensitive as well as ordinary, a fat man but, as he describes himself, "thin inside." The choice of such a man as his main character suggests a considerable increase in Orwell, between 1936 and 1938, of the common touch, a greater identification with the average person partly brought about by his experiences among north-country miners and in the egalitarian ranks of the Anarchist P.O.U.M. in Spain.

But although George Bowling's stance and personality are more relaxed than those of Orwell's earlier fictional protagonists, the situation in which he finds himself, between golden rural memories and the leaden, inescapable present, is one that Orwell described at the very start of his career as a novelist, when living in Hayes, on which Bowling's dreary suburb of "West Bletchley" is modeled.[40] In his poem "On a Ruined Farm near the His Master's Voice Gramophone Factory," which appeared in the *Adelphi* for April 1934, he explored his own predicament, stranded between the two "warring worlds" of agriculture and industrialism. Acknowledging, reluctantly, that the former was played out, no more than "weak and stuffless ghosts," he was nevertheless unable to give his allegiance, as others could, to the new landscape of "dizzy geometric towers" and "tapering cranes."[41] Four years later he was at once able to visualize the vanished past more sharply, and, while liking the present no better, was capable at least of stoicism. The "George" in George Bowling signals the predicament of the thirties—whether Fascist bombs or a debased life-style, which Bowling sums up as "bombs of filth exploding inside your mouth" (chap. 4)—as one that afflicted Orwell personally; but in giving his protagonist initials that also stand for "Great Britain," Orwell marks it as common property. Where the poem conveys an individual's sadness and bewilderment, the novel has something of the communal "grin and bear it" attitude, the solidarity in misfortune, that characterized Britain during World War II.

The presence of that attitude in the novel may have something to do with the circumstances in which it was written. Orwell's biographer, Bernard Crick, states that its "basic idea and structure" were in Orwell's mind by midsummer 1938, but he was unable to start writing it until the autumn.[42] In March 1938 he had experienced severe bleeding from a tuberculous lesion in the left lung, and spent from then until August in a sanitorium at Aylesford, near Maidstone in Kent. While recuperating there, he regularly went fishing, and in this renewal of one of the keenest pleasures of his own youth lies the origin of George Bowling's involvement with fishing, an experience that for him encapsulates an intensity of pleasure no longer possible in the modern world. Orwell did not begin writing, however, until he was settled in Marrakech, just under the High Atlas mountains in Morocco, where he had gone in September to continue his convalescence in a drier climate, aided by an anonymous gift of money from the novelist L. H. Myers. A diary entry made there on 13 November 1938 includes the phrase he was to use for the novel's title: "Tortoises . . . do not seem to stay under water very long without coming up for air."[43]

Orwell described the life and atmosphere of Marrakech itself only in a short, detached essay whose style resembles the coolness of Ernest Hemingway's.[44] What the place essentially gave him was a period of enforced separation from England, a literal breathing space that enabled him, like the tortoise, to surface and take stock of the past, though even that far off he was conscious, as he wrote to Cyril Connolly, that "everything one writes now is overshadowed by this ghastly feeling that we are rushing towards a precipice."[45] Occupying nearly all his time in Morocco, and written out of this intense and simultaneous awareness of past, present, and future, *Coming Up for Air* was finished just before Orwell sailed from Casablanca for London in March 1939. It was published in June, and though in 1948 Orwell spoke of it as having been pushed out of sight by the war,[46] it sold quite well, a further thousand copies being added in the same month to the two thousand originally printed. It provoked in the *Times Literary Supplement* the use for the first time of phrases that were to become virtually the trademark of response to Orwell's work: it was written, the anonymous reviewer noted, "with hard, honest clarity and precision of feeling,"[47] a remarkable compliment for a book that, more than any other by Orwell, relied on the intensity and accuracy of recollection.

Writing of Henry Miller's *Tropic of Cancer* in his essay "Inside the Whale" (1940), Orwell said that it read as if "the ordinary man, the 'average sensual man,' had been given the power of speech, like Balaam's ass."[48] He could have said much the same about *Coming Up for Air,* his only novel to employ a first-person narrator, who is first seen in the context of running bath water and a new set of false teeth, and last seen wondering how to placate the joyless wife who suspects he has been with another woman. Though not precisely the hen-pecked "little fat man" whose comic postcard existence Orwell studied in his essay "The Art of Donald McGill" (1942),[49] George Bowling has much in common with him, as well as with the lower-middle-class protagonists of H. G. Wells's novels, notably *The History of Mr. Polly* (1910), set in the Edwardian period to which Bowling's memories return in the second, longest, and most engrossing section of the novel.

"Wells watered down" was how Orwell described the novel in 1948, in a letter to Julian Symons. In the same letter he said that "one should never" write a novel in the first person.[50] The reason he gave was the constant intrusion of "my own character" into "that of the narrator"—something less irritating and more assimilable into the convention of fiction, one feels, than Orwell's authorial comments and "excess knowledge" as they occur in *Coming Up for Air*'s three third-person predecessors. Orwell repeated his objection in some manuscript notes, "For and against Novels in the First Person," he made in 1949;[51] but in developing it he reveals that the real limitation, for him, was not that the narrator would become too much like his author, but the reverse: "One's own comments unavoidably become those of the narrator!" That is, Orwell felt that the first-person method had restricted his freedom to make comments that the reader would recognize as specifically his.

It seems doubtful whether many readers would object to *Coming Up for Air* on these grounds.[52] Bowling's dislike of the "slick and shiny and streamlined" present (sect. 1, chap. 4), his nostalgic yet truthful evocation of the past, and his ability to recognize and face the future convey a clear emotional meaning, the respective contributions to which by narrator and author it does not seem vital to disentangle. Though Bernard Crick's praise of George Bowling as "a most subtle and well-rounded creation"[53] seems extravagant, the novel nevertheless does not prompt agreement with the quaintly doctrinaire position taken by Orwell in 1949: "in general an 'I' novel is simply the story of one person—a 3-dimensional figure among caricatures—and therefore cannot be a true novel."[54] *Coming Up for Air,* though indeed the story of one man, ranks next best to *Burmese Days* among Orwell's four novels with human characters and a "real" setting. It effectively exploits one of the "advantages" Orwell listed for the first-person novel, the ease with which the reader identifies with the narrator; even though not everything that happens to George Bowling seems quite as "credible," as authorially uncontrived, as Orwell believed the first-person novel was capable of making it.

Differentiated from Orwell at the outset of the novel by his lack of political commitment ("Down in Spain and over in China they were murdering one another as usual," Bowling remarks in the first chapter), Bowling nevertheless has "a kind of questioning attitude" implanted in him by the sizeable amount of reading he did while in a backwater army post during World War I; namely, Wells's *The History of Mr. Polly,* some Compton Mackenzie, Conrad's *Victory,* and some D. H. Lawrence (sec. 2, chap. 8). A short, fairly fat, fairly successful insurance salesman who describes himself as "vulgar" and "insensitive" and as fitting into his environment, he is also "thin inside," an introvert who recognizes "fear" as the element in which the human race now swims, and who at times has an acute prescience of the future as a world of posters, food queues, castor oil, rubber truncheons, and machine guns (sec. 1, chap. 4)—not precisely the world of Orwell's *Nineteen Eighty-Four,* but the decline that will precede it. A not entirely plausible assortment of characteristics, Bowling seems intended as a twentieth-century British Everyman, growing irritated rather than depressed by his life as a husband and father in a dull London suburb. Older than Orwell—forty-five to his thirty-five—Bowling is equipped with a longer reach of personal experience back into the past before the First World War, and it is this past into which the novel shows him escaping in its second and fourth sections, first through memory and then by means of his modest winnings on a horse race, which he has kept secret from his wife who, unlike him, has no "joy in life" or "any kind of interest in things for their own sake" (sec. 2, chap. 10). The contrast between present and past provides the plotless *Coming Up for Air* with its tension, and the detailed recreation of the past contributes the real strength of the novel; though it is a strength of a kind incapable of arresting the world's movement toward war, announced in section 1 by the bombing plane that keeps pace with Bowling's train into central London.

Bowling's plunge into the past that, suddenly enveloping him, seems more real than the present, comes about through an instantaneous verbal association: the sight of a newspaper headline about King Zog of Albania returns him to his hometown, Lower Binfield, in 1900, the smell of its parish church, and the sound of two local tradesmen antiphonally booming out verses of the psalms about "Sihon King of the Amorites and Og the King of Bashan."[55] This vivid reexperiencing of the past leads directly to the ten chapters of section 2, in which Bowling recalls his early years as the son of a small corn merchant, and the changes after the Great War that brought him to a kind of suburban life—a house with a bathroom, a higher-class wife, a job in insurance, a car—which his father would think "wonderful," but which is a poor exchange for a rural childhood spent in "real air" and remembered as perpetual summer. Orwell's own view of the relevance of Bowling's recollections is made clear by the latter's direct challenge to readers of his own generation: "Is it gone for good? I'm not certain. But I tell you it was a good world to live in. I belong to it. So do you" (448).

Lower Binfield, an imaginary town near the Thames in Oxfordshire, cannot be exactly pinpointed as Orwell's Shiplake and Henley, but there is no doubt that Bowling's "total recall" owes much to Orwell's own childhood.[56] The detailed parade of facts, folklore, smells, tastes, sights, and experiences makes up a tour-de-force, impossible to summarize adequately, in which Orwell's own memories and his imaginative empathy can scarcely be separated. What essentially comes across is the "difference" of the Edwardian past, which possessed a slowness, a peacefulness, and an excitement that was focused for Bowling in his experience of fishing, and in the very "names of English coarse fish." It was the "fishing" parts of the work that Orwell told Julian Symons he had especially wanted to write, and Bowling's question "Where are the English coarse fish now?" has all the plangency of Villon's famous ballade, with its refrain "Ou sont les neiges d'antan?"—"Where are the snows of yesteryear?"

Nevertheless, the picture that Bowling, and through him Orwell, presents is far from an idealized golden innocence, "that poetry of childhood stuff" (472). Two details of it—Bowling and his peers stamping on half-fledged chicks for fun, and blowing up toads with a bicycle pump until they burst—point up the realism of the book's approach, palliated only by a comment attached to the second: "That's what boys are like, I don't know why"(469). Bowling's view of childhood is far from Wordsworthian: "A boy isn't interested in meadows, groves and so forth . . . killing things,—that's about as near to poetry as a boy gets" (472). The reader may protest that "the child is father to the man," yet any implication here that such boyhood acts lead logically to bombing planes and other inhumanity seems unintended by narrator and author alike, and is too fleeting to undermine the persuasiveness of the book's overall pattern of contrast. Though Bowling's early world offered many of its denizens a harsh life for little financial reward, it also gave them "a feeling of security . . . more exactly . . . continuity" (493) not to be found in the present. For Bowling—and Orwell offers no qualification of this attitude—nostalgia for "my own particular childhood," with its "peculiar intensity," is inseparable from a "sentimental" feeling about "the civilisation which I grew up in and which is now, I suppose, just about at its last kick" (473). It is not just subjective childhood that is better, but the objective past, a past that, once "as permanent . . . as the pyramids," vanished for Bowling with the death of his parents during World War I, to whose home he has never since returned, and which, until the accidental jogging of his memory in a London street, has ceased to be alive in his mind.

Two different sorts of pressure, demonstrated in section 3, combine to decide Bowling to spend his horse-race winnings on a brief return trip to Lower Binfield. One is created by a meeting of the West Bletchley branch of the Left Book Club, where a vehement invited speaker warns the small audience about "The Menace of Fascism." This inspires in Bowling less a fear of fascism itself than a sense of the unavoidable "hate, hate, hate" being fomented on both sides of the political divide of the 1930s, and a foreboding not so much of war as of what will follow it: a world that, like the hate, anticipates Orwell's fuller vision in *Nineteen Eighty-Four.* He derives no comfort from a visit afterwards to his friend Porteous, a retired public schoolmaster uninterested in the modern world; Bowling suddenly sees him, without hostility, as a "ghost," a representative of "the old, nice world that can't see what's coming" (525). The only choice for Bowling's generation seems an impossible one, between "dead men and live gorillas." A later encounter, however, with a field of primroses in warm spring weather, brings him a rush of happiness akin, in secular terms, to that felt by Dorothy Hare early in *A Clergyman's Daughter.* Aware of the imminence of war and what it will bring, Bowling determines to experience such "peace" more fully, by "coming up for air" in Lower Binfield.

His few days there, described in section 4, are a sequence of anticlimax, poignant and bewildering for him, but for the reader too predictable and underlined too heavily. Coming to his birthplace by his boyhood route from the Thames, he cannot recognize it. The old town of two thousand people has simply been "swallowed" by a new one of twenty-five thousand working in light industry and living in new-looking public housing. His old home is now the quaint "Wendy's Teashop"; all the old familiar names are off the shop fronts and on gravestones; the girl he once loved has become "a round-shouldered hag, shambling along on twisted heels" (553), barely recognizable herself and unable to recognize Bowling, who realizes that here he is a ghost like Porteous. The Thames, once "a luminous green that you could see deep into" (551), is now crowded, brown, and dirty; and when—his last hope—he goes to the hidden pool near Binfield House to try to catch one of the enormous carp he had glimpsed there as a boy, he finds that the house is now a mental institution and the pool has turned into a garbage dump. His climactic outburst blends the sense of loss with the recognition of reality: "What's the good of trying to revisit the scenes of your boyhood? They don't exist. Coming up for air! But there isn't any air. The dustbin that we're in reaches up to the stratosphere" (560). As if to drive home the lesson, a plane on a training mission from a nearby airbase accidentally drops a bomb, killing three people and bringing out into the street a group of children who, running in their gas masks, give Bowling for one grotesque moment the illusion of "a herd of pigs."

From this point the novel moves hastily to its conclusion. Convinced now that "there'll be no more fishing this side of the grave" (564), and recognizing the bomb as not only "terrible," but "real" (a link reflective of Orwell's own psyche), Bowling returns home to his neglected family responsibilities and the anger of his wife, from whom he has concealed the true reason for his absence by an elaborate but predictably doomed stratagem. Hardly able, now, to explain his compulsion to revisit Lower Binfield to himself, let alone to her, he prefers to let her believe he wasted his money on a woman rather than on a foolish but imaginative exercise in nostalgia.

The rapid shifts of tone in the novel's last chapter suggest that Orwell was anxious to complete the book before he left Morocco. The ending is abrupt, messy, and disappointing, as if the author, having reanimated the past with considerable power and then replaced it with the vision of an irreversible present, had little further use for the inquisitive and sensitive aspects of his narrator, and wished to have done with him. Though Bowling's turning away from disappointed dreams of the past can be seen, in character terms, as a reassertion of his common sense, it has the effect of suddenly bursting a fictional balloon that Orwell has taken great pains to inflate. Viewed so many years after the two historical periods it contrasts, *Coming Up for Air* now seems most powerful in its second section, as an evocation of the distant past, a densely detailed sociological record of childhood and youth in the Edwardian age, convincingly embodied as one memorable character's story. In the sense it also gives, perhaps no more than incidentally, of the persistence of the past in some dimension impervious to time and accessible to memory, the novel merits interest as Orwell's only treatment of a "highbrow" literary topic. For Orwell himself, finishing it early in 1939, it seems most likely that *Coming Up for Air* represented both a retrospection and a clearing for action before the last remnants of the old world were swept away. Less than three weeks after it was published, the Second World War began.

Chapter Four

Men and Brothers

Through the character of George Bowling, Orwell conveyed the part of himself that, feeling unable to deflect the future, longed unavailingly to recapture the past. He had, however, clearly acknowledged the necessity of becoming involved with the present, and shared with W. H. Auden, one of the "nancy poets" he so much disparaged at this time, the notion of "Today, the struggle."[1] For Auden, as for so many writers of the 1930s, this imperative was the message of the Spanish Civil War, which began in July 1936. Orwell too was one of those writers; when, in 1946, he came to consider the mixed motives that impel an author, he attributed the preeminence in his own work of the political impulse to "the Spanish war and other events in 1936–7," after which all his "serious" work had "been written, directly or indirectly, *against* totalitarianism and *for* democratic socialism."[2] For Orwell, the other events were his visits, in succession, to various depressed areas in northern England, which took place in the winter months of early 1936, and led to his first politically "committed" piece of extended writing, *The Road to Wigan Pier* (1937).

This book and its successor, *Homage to Catalonia* (1938), have given rise, more than any other of his works, to the view of Orwell as a champion of truth, decency, and justice in a world of privilege and oppression, and as a man who risked health and life in his identification with the struggles of the workers. There is much in both books that justifies such a view, but it is worth remembering that they did not come into being in the same way. Whereas Orwell's journey to Spain, like those of many of his literary contemporaries, was made by his own choice, and his book about it achieved publication with difficulty and sold slowly, Orwell's visit to northern England was undertaken at his publisher's suggestion and subsidized by an unusually large advance of five hundred pounds—as much money as Orwell could then expect to earn in two years. The resultant book, by concentrating at least in part 1 entirely on what Orwell found in the North, forces the reader to attend to unpleasant realities; but by omitting all reference to what provoked its author to go there it may have suggested to its very large Left Book Club audience, for whom 43,690 copies were printed, that Orwell had lived among miners and the unemployed solely because of internal compulsion.[3] One may feel, too, that the personal treatment that Orwell weaves into part 2 of the book partakes as much of "sheer egoism"[4] as of a wish to be honest about middle-class origins and the obstacles they set up to Socialist solidarity.

The Road to Wigan Pier (1937)

Orwell went north at the end of January 1936, and returned to London at the end of March. Five weeks of this two-month period were almost equally divided between the medium-sized coal-mining towns of Wigan in Lancashire and Barnsley in Yorkshire, where there was much unemployment; the rest of it was used for short visits to the mercantile and industrial cities of Liverpool, Manchester, and Sheffield ("one of the most appalling places I have ever seen"),[5] and to the home of Orwell's married sister Marjorie in Leeds. In Wigan, Barnsley, and Sheffield, Orwell stayed with working-class people; in Leeds, Manchester, and Liverpool, where he was recovering from a bout of bronchitis perhaps brought on by his exhausting first exploration of a coal mine, he stayed in middle-class homes.

Few of the circumstantial details of Orwell's trip—what happened where, how he got from place to place, the various people he met and stayed with and who expedited his inquiries—found their way into the finished book. It is possible to reconstruct the progress of his journey, and its full scope, only from recently published reminiscences by acquaintances,[6] and from an early, chronological, version of Orwell's experiences that, when printed in 1968, was given the title "'The Road to Wigan Pier' Diary."[7] To attend too much to this here would be to swing the emphasis unduly from the literary to the biographical, but some reference must be made to it, since what Orwell omitted from his final, published version helps in the assessment of what he left in it, transposed, and added to it.

Orwell's omission from *The Road to Wigan Pier* of his actual journey north—by train to Coventry in the Midlands, then a hundred or so miles on foot—may have resulted from his wishing to conform to his brief from Victor Gollancz: this, according to Bernard Crick, was "to write a book about the condition of the unemployed in the industrial areas in the north of England."[8] If so, however, Orwell was not consistent: the self-revelation and political criticism that make up part 2 of the book are also outside his brief, and were retained in the large Left Book Club printing against Gollancz's opposition. The journey omitted, the published book opens in medias res, as if to allow the reader no escape into a wider context; the mention of "mill-girls' clogs" and "factory whistles which I was never awake to hear" establishes, for British readers at least, a generic northern location. It also unobtrusively indicates the unoccupied narrator's apartness from working-class routine. Yet though the ensuing description of Orwell's overcrowded, smelly lodgings in a tripe shop has become celebrated for its depiction of dreariness and squalor, the "slice of life" it presents seems like a held-over episode from *Down and Out in Paris and London* rather than, to judge from local comments after the book appeared, a representative sample of Wigan proletarian life. "It is a kind of duty to see and smell such places now and again," Orwell wrote in chapter 1; but by choosing to stay at the tripe shop he was fulfilling a duty to himself rather than to his readers.

It is noticeable that the use of place names, normal throughout the "Diary," coincides in the book more often with brief comments and statistical references than with carefully described scenes; as a result one has a paradoxical sense of small, vivid particulars located in no precise geography. The coal mine that Orwell depicts with such muscular immediacy in chapter 2 resembles "my own mental picture of hell," but he feels it unnecessary to mention which of the three mines he went down in Wigan and Barnsley this one is.[9] Not until the end of chapter 3, in fact, does any place name occur.

Along with this geographical imprecision goes a thinness of human reference, especially noticeable when one compares Orwell's book with J. B. Priestley's *English Journey* (1934), whose warmth of human concern, particularly demonstrated in relation to conditions in the depressed areas of northeastern England, quickly made it a classic of social reporting. Though Orwell's presentation of the kind of life led by miners, and the problems, such as inadequate wages, the dole, and housing, faced by the northern working class is conscientious, involving, and often moving, there are few detailed studies of individuals, and no reference whatever, whether for contrast or to state frankly Orwell's foothold in a very different world, to the middle-class people he encountered in the North: trades union officials, members of the Independent Labour Party, contacts provided by the *Adelphi,* his own relatives in Leeds. One of the few paragraphs concerned with an individual coincides with the first mention of Wigan by name at the end of chapter 3. It presents a miner badly afflicted by nystagmus. Orwell's concentration on the miner's condition, and on the inconvenience to which he was subjected in order to draw his inadequate disability pension (184), is understandable, and there is no doubting Orwell's dissatisfaction with the system's ungenerous treatment of one of its faithful servants. Yet Orwell gives no indication of the miner's own opinion or feelings; he remains an object rather than a subject. Even when Orwell conveys his admiration for the strength and the splendid physique of miners (chap. 2),[10] they come over as types rather than as people: one part of Orwell speaks of their "arms and belly-muscles of steel," while another pities them as "poor drudges." But no part of Orwell seems to present them as men with interests that might diversify or palliate their lives, or with souls, perhaps, that might transcend them. It is noticeable that whereas, in the "Diary" Orwell speaks of having gone down the Wigan coal mine with seven particular people,[11] in *The Road to Wigan Pier* he mentions only one, and only in general terms: "your guide, a miner, is sympathetic."(171). The overall effect of this "editing out" is to appropriate experience for Orwell, and for the reader at his back, but by reducing the reader's sense of its context to give it an overdramatic element of claustrophobia. This is partly a function of the middle-class outsider in Orwell, which he admits in part 2; and also of his awareness, discussed in chapter 7, of the "difference" of the North, which he had never previously visited and knew little of.

Orwell's treatment of his material is, indeed, highly selective. He attended political meetings of varying stripe,[12] but while they had some effect on his theorizing in part 2 he omits any reference to them as events. Only the briefest mention is made of Liverpool, though in his few days there he visited docks and slums and corporation rehousing schemes. Nor does he refer to his meeting there with the unemployed Communist docker George Garrett, who had contributed short stories to the *Adelphi* under the pseudonym "Matt Lowe"; an interesting omission in view of Orwell's assertion in part 2, chapter 11, that "it is doubtful whether anything describable as proletarian literature now exists." It was generous of Walter Greenwood, the working-class author of *Love on the Dole* (1933), to ignore this generalization in his appreciative review of *The Road to Wigan Pier* in *Tribune*;[13] especially generous in that Orwell refers in passing to the dramatized version of that novel in chapter 5. In view of the fact that only half of Orwell's book consists of direct reportage of "the condition of the unemployed in the North of England," omissions of this sort become all the more puzzling; it seems as if Orwell were deliberately leaving the maximum room for his own revelations, reflections, and exhortations in part 2.

In the course of the book's composition, Orwell described it to Jack Common as "a sort of book of essays,"[14] and this is certainly true of part 1. Undoubtedly the most powerful "essay" is Orwell's description (chap. 2) of going down a mine, with its revelation not only of the hard labor of coal-getting amid constant heat, noise, and dust, but of the great distances—from one to three miles—that miners had to "travel" underground, often stooping or crawling and always unpaid, since "travelling" did not count as work, to reach the coal face. In chapter 13 of *English Journey* Priestley had felt no need to describe a coal mine, "as everybody at some time or other must have read a detailed account" of one.[15] Whatever these unnamed accounts were, Orwell's has long since supplanted them.

Chapter 3 supplements Orwell's account, admiring and horrified at once, with general details of the miner's life that accumulate to suggest the ingratitude with which he is treated by society, and the unfairness of middle-class assumptions about him. Among other things, Orwell points out the comparative rarity of pit-head baths, an amenity paid for less by the colliery owners than out of miners' own welfare fund contributions; the inconvenience of shift changes to miners and their families; the smallness of a miner's net wages (an average of £105 a year after various "stoppages," including one for the hire of the lamp essential to his work) compared with his coal production of some 280 tons a year; and the many occupational hazards—gas explosions, collapsing galleries, the occasional plunge of a cage at top speed to the bottom of a shaft—that made mining more dangerous than any other job.

Three of the remaining chapters are taken up, in turn, with housing, unemployment, and details of working-class diet. Housing was inadequate in both quantity and quality; masses of dwellings, old, ugly, and insanitary, that had officially been condemned as unfit for human habitation were still standing, and in Wigan Orwell discovered a squalid settlement of fixed caravans that reminded him of coolies' huts in Burma. Orwell was concerned not only to provide statistics of measurements and rents, and to explain to middle-class readers the meaning of terms like "one up, one down" and "back to back," but to make them grasp the misery involved in actually living in such places, particularly on inadequate public assistance. In this he is certainly successful. But it was a curious oversight of his publisher that the thirty-two depressing photographs with which *The Road to Wigan Pier* was illustrated came from not a single place that Orwell had actually visited.[16]

In revealing the realities of life on the dole, Orwell was quick to point out the absurdity—frequent among the southern middle classes—of expecting people to look for work when there plainly was none, and he drew attention to the "frightful feeling of impotence and despair, which is about the worst evil of unemployment." He felt, however, that the unemployed were getting more used to their condition, making it more bearable by "lowering their standards"; this was hardly a desirable situation, but had to be expected in a law-abiding country (chap. 5). One of the palliatives to despair that Orwell characteristically noticed was the working-class liking for cheap foods that were "tasty" rather than "wholesome"; in comparing an unemployed miner's food budget with a list of more sensible expenditures Orwell commented that "the ordinary human being would sooner starve than live on brown bread and raw carrots" (chap. 6). Nevertheless he could not fail to see the bad teeth and deteriorating physiques that were resulting from an understandable proletarian reluctance to follow the pious advice of people who did not know what poverty felt like.

Orwell closes his account of the North proper with a curious chapter that, emphasizing the division between North and South established by the Industrial Revolution, moves from initial horror at the North's ugly landscape of "flashes" and slagheaps, and irritation at the North's view of its superior "grit," to praise for the northern working classes. Intimacy with them, he felt, was impossible; but they had welcomed him politely, and he had come to admire their family loyalty and their commonsense view of education ("why stay at school after 14"?), and to feel that "there is much in middle-class life that looks sickly and debilitating when you see it from a working-class angle" (chap. 7). This rosy view culminates in what has become a locus classicus in Orwell commentary: his picture of a working-class interior in which father "reading the racing finals," mother sewing, and the children eating mint humbugs relax along with the family dog in front of a glowing fire (228). Orwell suggests both the preciousness and the precariousness of this scene, poised between the grinding, superstitious Middle Ages and the eugenic metal utopias of the future, and only possible when "father is in work." But this caveat is less emphasized than it might be, and such an idealizing end to a fact-finding tour is surely too subtle to prick the reader's conscience. It contrasts strangely with another locus classicus of the book; his description, leaving Wigan by train, of seeing a young woman, kneeling "on the slimy stones of a slum backyard," trying to clear a blocked waste pipe in bitter weather, and wearing "the most desolate, hopeless expression I have ever seen" (chap. 1). In the "Diary" Orwell encounters the woman when walking up an alley.[17] It is strange that Orwell should not have sharpened the effect of the altered scene further by placing it at the end of part 1 as an example of the opposite end of the working-class spectrum: the victim whose inability to escape from the environment accuses both the departing observer and the cushioned middle-class reader.

Part 1 of *The Road to Wigan Pier* continues to have documentary interest as a record of what one part of England was like during the depression. The polemical part 2, which Orwell felt might disqualify the book as a choice for the Left Book Society started by Gollancz, Harold Laski, and John Strachey in May 1936, has worn less well, half of it representing, essentially, a record of Orwell's struggle with his own class prejudices, much of the rest expressing his reservations about the mechanized future to which socialism seemed to be leading, and his irritation with the "unsatisfactory and inhuman types" to whom theoretical socialism seemed to appeal (chap. 11). Gollancz felt it necessary to write a foreword in which he dissociated himself from many of Orwell's highly provocative statements in order to disclaim responsibility for the offense he rightly foresaw they would cause in socialist circles,[18] despite Orwell's affirmation near the end that only socialism, properly humanized, could "save us from the misery of the present or the nightmare of the future" (292). Among various confusions in the book, Gollancz shrewdly pointed out the contradiction between Orwell's picture of three-roomed houses in which it was hard "to keep anything decent" when there were masses of children (chap. 4), and his hostility to socialist "birth-control fanatics" (chap. 12).

Half of part 2 shows Orwell facing the snobbery and class division that prevented an effective uniting of bourgeoisie and proletariat to deal with the problems presented in part 1. In using his own earlier life as an exemplary middle-class case, he incidentally reveals the full point of his book's title. "Wigan Pier" was no more than a jetty, by then demolished, on the Leeds and Liverpool Canal; the term was used sardonically by locals to denote the gap between inland, industrial

Wigan and the resorts on the Lancashire coast to which they might aspire when fully employed. Orwell presented his "road" to it as a kind of expiatory pilgrimage, intending the phrase to contrast with the Kiplingesque "road to Mandalay" he had mistakenly taken as an imperial policeman. Since that time, realizing that "the upper-middle-class is done for" (chap. 8), he had tried to overcome the prejudices of his "shabby-genteel" upbringing—among them the widespread notion that "the lower classes smell"—and get closer to the working class, his encounters with tramps being only an intermediate stage. Orwell presented the difficulties of class adjustment with intelligence and honesty: he was well aware that "to abolish class-distinctions means to abolish part of yourself" (chap. 10), and felt that the cant and hostility that existed on both sides could not be removed overnight.

But if there ever were to be a closing of ranks against the inroads of fascism, which Orwell feared was becoming not only more powerful but more popular, socialism needed to put its house in order, and the last three chapters of the book suggest—naively in the view of left-wing theoretician Harold Laski[19]—what was wrong with it and what might be done. For Orwell, who attended the Independent Labour Party Summer School in Letchworth in July 1936, two months after beginning to write the book, too many socialists were "cranks" of one kind or another (his list in chap. 11 gave great offense, and is uncomfortably close to an intolerant catalog of personal dislikes); moreover, many were "mingy little beasts," too concerned to cling to "their miserable fragments of social prestige." The ordinary worker, for whom, as for Orwell, socialism meant "justice and common decency" and a real wish "to see tyranny overthrown," was merely put off by them. More important, the aims of theoretical socialism, as Orwell saw them—to bring about a Brave New World in which such admirable human qualities as courage and effort would become redundant—were spiritually repellent to a wider range of people: to the working class because such people envisaged a socialist world as like the present one, but "with the worst abuses left out" (chap. 11), and to more educated people because they valued the notions of discipline and tradition that fascism was all too capable of harnessing.

To these problems, the correctness of whose diagnosis was much argued over when *The Road to Wigan Pier* was published in March 1937, Orwell was able to offer only tentative solutions. But though his analysis of the problems—subjective, confused, sympathetic, intemperate—diminished in interest as the period to which it related faded into history, his suggestions for dealing with them retain a force based on their appeal to deep-seated human notions of tolerance and fair play. For Orwell, socialism needed to become less chillingly utopian, "a league of the oppressed against the oppressors" in which "there is room for human beings" (chap. 13). For socialism to be effective, the working class and "the exploited middle class," each starting with a careful tolerance of the other's special characteristics and differences, had gradually to come together, learning in the fight against "plutocracy" and authoritarianism that they had more in common than they thought. According to the Communist Manifesto of 1848, the workers had "nothing to lose but their chains"; in the jaunty words of Orwell's allusive final phrase, the middle classes to which he belonged had "nothing to lose but our aitches."

When he had finished *The Road to Wigan Pier* in December 1936, Orwell had not quite succeeded in linking the eloquence of his peroration with his picture of working-class conditions, left behind at the end of part 1. The hyperbole of his last minute reference to socialism's need to save "the twenty million Englishmen whose bones are rotting from malnutrition" (chap. 13) jibes oddly with his failure to send any copies of his book to those working-class individuals in Wigan and elsewhere who had helped him.[20] By the time he returned to England in the summer of 1937, his experiences of nonmetaphorical fighting against fascism, in Spain, had brought the wish to sink "into the working class where we belong" (chap. 13) closer to becoming a reality.

Homage to Catalonia (1938)

Orwell wrote *The Road to Wigan Pier* in Wallington, a tiny village set in attractive rolling arable country five miles from Baldock in Hertfordshire. He moved there at the beginning of April, just after his return from the North, renting a primitive but cheap cottage whose earlier function as a shop was revived in a small way by himself and Eileen O'Shaughnessy, whom he married on 9 June 1936 in the village church. This remote and simple life—Orwell writing through the summer and autumn, planting vegetables and keeping a goat, his wife looking after the house and selling sweets to the village children—seems to have suited him, perhaps because in it he could unite the industry of the worker with the independence and self-sufficiency of the aristocracy from which his family was descended. It was a way of life he was to choose again after World War II, when he went to live in the extreme agrarian remoteness of the island of Jura, off the west coast of Scotland.

Orwell lived in Wallington, on and off, until May 1940. His first period there, however, lasted no longer than the time it took him to complete his book on his experiences in the North. Immediately after it was finished he left for Spain, traveling during the Christmas holiday, via Paris, and arriving in Barcelona by train on 26 December 1936. The Spanish Civil War had started that July with the revolt of the right-wing Nationalist forces under General Franco against the elected Republican government, which by now retained control of no more than half of Spain, a portion that ran irregularly inland from the Mediterranean and just included the capital, Madrid, which fell only a few days before the war ended in March 1939.

Orwell's own involvement in the war, which included over four months' active service on the Aragon front between Saragossa and Huesca, lasted from the end of 1936 to the end of June 1937. By that time he had been hit in the throat by a sniper's bullet, but he had also gained two contrasting realizations: a firm commitment to democratic socialism, and the understanding that the conflict in which he had joined was a far more complex matter than his initial idealism had supposed. At the end of *Homage to Catalonia* he notes with evident sincerity that "curiously enough the whole experience has left me with not less but more belief in the decency of human beings."[21] "Curiously" is the operative word: it is easy to imagine someone less resilient, less determined to see the good in humanity, being totally disillusioned after the experiences Orwell's book describes. This disillusionment would not have been prompted by Orwell's experiences at the front, where the atmosphere was one of proletarian solidarity; but by the cynical political maneuverings that accompanied the struggle between the various left-wing factions, and by the gradual choking out (in the cause of military efficiency) of the "revolutionary atmosphere" (chap. 8, 379) that still prevailed in Barcelona when he arrived there. Orwell had expressed to Philip Mairet, editor of the *New English Weekly,* his reason for going in the stirring words: "This Fascism . . . someone's got to stop it."[22] The difference between Orwell's arrival as a volunteer to fight fascism and his departure six months later as a proscribed "Trotskyite" fugitive is sharply summed up in his remark in the last chapter of his book, that to enter Catalonia you had to look proletarian, but to leave it you had to look bourgeois. In the interval, what had been stopped was not fascism but what from Orwell's perspective appeared to be "a foretaste of Socialism" (chap. 8) of a genuinely classless sort.

Though he shared with many of his literary contemporaries the impulse to participate in the civil war, Orwell's perspective on it was an unusual one, and not only because, unlike W. H. Auden and Stephen Spender, he was a combatant rather than a medical auxiliary or an observer. Even as a combatant he differed from the young poet John Cornford, a convinced Communist who died fighting with the Communist-organized International Brigade near Cordoba at the end of 1936. His difference stemmed from his factional affiliation, whose significance he did not at first understand, as he makes clear in chapter 5 of *Homage to Catalonia,* the first of two "political chapters" that interrupt, and shed light on, the linear narrative of his experiences: "When I came to Spain and for some time afterwards, I was not only uninterested in the political situation but unaware of it. . . . If you had asked me why I had joined the militia I should have answered: 'To fight against fascism,' and if you had asked me what I was fighting *for,* I should have answered 'Common decency'" (333). At this time Orwell assumed that all who were fighting fascism were "Socialists," and was impatient with the "plague of initials" that in fact represented a wide range of very different left-wing parties: the Anarcho-Syndicalist C.N.T. (the largest workers' union), the Communist P.S.U.C., and the Anarchist P.O.U.M., whose zeal for social reform on egalitarian lines was the purest—or most extreme—in the whole spectrum of groups lined up, and jostling for power, behind the Republican government.

Having gone to Spain under the auspices of the Independent Labour Party, it was to its Spanish equivalent, the P.O.U.M. (*Partido Obrero de Unificacion Marxista,* or Workers' Party of Marxist Unity) that Orwell naturally gravitated, joining its ill-equipped and ill-disciplined militia a few days after arriving in Barcelona and soon finding himself, ironically because of his experience in the Eton Officer Training Corps and the Burma police, a corporal with little Spanish in charge of twelve Spaniards. Eventually, in his last ten days of active service before being wounded, he became the equivalent of a second lieutenant, in charge of a platoon of ILP volunteers.

Orwell's initial irritation with the P.O.U.M's lack of modern weapons (his own rifle was a forty-year-old model), the impractical drilling in the Lenin Barracks that passed for "instruction," and the unmilitary reluctance of the militia volunteers to obey orders without arguing, together with his early front-line experience in which "there seemed no hope of any real fighting" (chap. 4), led to a growing wish to transfer to the far more active Madrid front, the responsibility of the International Brigade. This would have involved acceding to the Communist view that radical social change—implemented by the Anarchists in the Aragon countryside and in their egalitarian militia units—needed to be postponed in order to win the war, which the Communists, and the central government, felt could be done only by absorbing the various militia into a "Popular Army" with a hierarchical command structure and unquestioning obedience. Despite Orwell's initial warm, if confused, response to the egalitarian euphoria of semi-autonomous Catalonia—a state of affairs he did not altogether like but "recognised . . . immediately as . . . worth fighting for" (chap. 1)—Orwell nevertheless sympathized for a time with the more militarily efficient Communist viewpoint.

This attitude shifted, however, when he returned to Barcelona late in April 1937, after 115 days in the line, to find that "the revolutionary atmosphere had vanished" (chap. 9), a change he significantly compared to arriving in the cool privileged hill station of Maymyo in Upper Burma after a train journey from the heat and jostling of Mandalay. Class divisions had returned; working-class areas experienced food shortages unknown in the expensive restaurants; cabarets and brothels (originally closed by workers' patrols) had reopened; and smartly uniformed officers of the new "Popular Army" were walking the streets sporting automatic pistols unobtainable on the Aragon front, whose lack of modern weapons was at least partly attributable to the factional rivalry of the Communists, who controlled the distribution of arms supplied by Russia.

With Russian intervention, Communist influence on the Madrid government had enormously increased, and that influence Orwell had come to see as exerted not to help the social revolution, which inside Spain "nobody doubted was going on" (chap. 5), but to bring it to a halt. When street fighting broke out in May between Anarchist workers and the government's Civil Guards, sent to take over the Barcelona telephone exchange, for Orwell the larger ideological rivalries of the left boiled down to a simple gut response: in the clash between workers and the police, it was the workers with whom he sided. When, in the following month, intensifying P.S.U.C. propaganda led to the suppression of the P.O.U.M. as a "Trotskyite Fifth column working for Franco" (an accusation the Republican government repudiated six months after Orwell's book appeared), Orwell's disgust with Communist smear tactics and his distress at the widespread arrests to which they gave rise, predictably led him to prefer the underdog P.O.U.M. with whom he had fought; so that *Homage to Catalonia* not only describes his own eyewitness involvement in the Barcelona "troubles" but adopts a point of view essentially sympathetic to the Anarchists who had been "systematically denigrated" in the world press. "As I know by my own experience," Orwell wrote in chapter 11, "it is almost impossible to get anyone to print anything in their defence." Orwell's biggest "experience"[23] of this kind had been with Victor Gollancz, who had declined to publish Orwell's book on Spain immediately on discovering, before it was written, that Orwell had fought with the P.O.U.M. Instead, *Homage to Catalonia* was published in April 1938 by the newly established left-wing firm of Secker and Warburg.

Hugh Thomas, in his monumental history of the civil war published in 1961, stated that *Homage to Catalonia* is "a better book about war itself than about the Spanish War."[24] From such an authority, with access to Spanish printed sources and to all angles of the war, this opinion carries weight. Orwell's account of the various left-wing factions in chapter 5, and his attempt in chapter 11 "to try to establish the truth" of the Barcelona street fighting of May 1937 by "diving into the cesspool" of conflicting views, are as factually accurate as his knowledge could make them: and chapter 11 is remarkably restrained and benevolent when one considers the vilification of the P.O.U.M. in the foreign and Spanish communist press that it is concerned to refute. Nevertheless, Orwell felt it necessary to "warn everyone against my bias" in chapter 11, and a complete, objective picture of the Spanish war, whether militarily or politically, can only be obtained from the records of historians, which it is beyond the scope of this study to subsume.

But such necessary historical reservations do not reduce the power of Orwell's book, either as a depiction of one man's experience of war or as the large-scale embodiment of a sensation that Orwell encapsulates in one sentence in chapter 8: "One had been in a community where hope was more normal than apathy or cynicism, where the word 'comrade' stood for comradeship and not, as in most countries, for humbug." As his political awareness increased, Orwell came to realize that, in fighting on the Aragon front, he had been "more or less by chance . . . isolated among the most revolutionary section of the Spanish working class" (chap. 5). There, and in his first short period in Barcelona, he had had a rare opportunity to breathe "the air of equality" (chap. 8), of whose brief existence his book, with its accurately restricted title, is a moving record. Characteristically, writing to Jack Common early in 1938, Orwell said that the title of his recently completed book "will be *Homage to Catalonia,* because we couldn't think of a better one."[25] In fact, no better one could have been chosen: as well as being an account of events now "receded into enormous distance" the book is an elegiac tribute to a perished ideal.

Much of the power of *Homage to Catalonia,* in contrast to *The Road to Wigan Pier,* derives from its straightforward linear structure. Orwell chose to open the book with an incident that, though factual, and though it occurred early in his Spanish experience, seems to have been selected more for its emblematic value—Orwell's brief "meeting in utter intimacy" with a fierce, illiterate young Italian militiaman who gripped his hand in proletarian solidarity, and who symbolized for Orwell all the bright prospects of a better society that seemed to be opening in Barcelona late in 1936. Six years later, he concluded his retrospective essay "Looking Back on the Spanish War" (1943) with a poem he had written in that militiaman's memory "when the war was visibly lost" by the end of 1938. The poem lacks technical polish but it well conveys Orwell's feelings of comradeship, and his bitterness at the betrayal and death, not only of the anonymous militiaman, but of named Spaniards also encountered at the Lenin Barracks. Like *Homage to Catalonia,* the poem ends with an assertion of human survival in the face of defeat, though the undeniable force of the word "crystal" is at odds with the physical context in which it functions as a metaphor:

> But the thing I saw in your face
> No power can disinherit:
> No bomb that ever burst
> Shatters the crystal spirit.[26]

But unlike the mill-girls in *The Road to Wigan Pier,* whose clogs provide its opening sound, the militiaman, however briefly encountered, is described in some detail and placed in a specific geographical context. This precision of treatment characterizes the rest of *Homage to Catalonia,* which Bernard Crick has correctly called "closer to a literal record than anything [Orwell] wrote."[27] The names used by Orwell, of soldiers no less than of politicians, are all real ones, there is eyewitness confirmation for all the main incidents and Orwell consistently indicates where he is, as well as what he and others are doing. Part of the reason for Orwell's accuracy was, no doubt, that Spain was a foreign country and readers could not be expected to know their way around it, either politically or geographically. But the clarity of Orwell's narrative has also a haunting, even a romantic quality that suggests he wished to "fix" his experiences before they faded. Though the realities of Orwell's war were mainly undramatic,—a struggle with boredom, cold, and discomfort in which "nothing ever happened" (chap. 6) and "firewood, food, tobacco, candles and the enemy" were important in that order (chap. 3)—his weeks as a comrade in "a sort of temporary working model of the classless society" affected him more sharply than his role as an observer in northern England; he himself speaks of their "curious vividness" (chap. 8). In addition to this, he not surprisingly responded more strongly to the pristine Spanish landscape than to the industry-scarred terrain around Wigan: the mountain scenery on the Aragon front was "stupendous" (chap. 3), and "the growing light and seas of carmine cloud stretching away into inconceivable distances" made it "almost worth while" to be up so often in the cold dawn (chap. 4). The coming together of stirring historical occasion and striking physical location is most memorably caught in his description of his arrival, wounded, in Tarragona just in time to see another train pulling out. It was packed with Italians of the International Brigade, bound for the Aragon front where most of them were to die fighting at Huesca soon after:

> I remember with particular vividness the spectacle of that train passing in the yellow evening light; window after window full of dark smiling faces, the long tilted barrels of the guns, the scarlet scarves fluttering—all this gliding slowly past against a turquoise-coloured sea. . . . It was like an allegorical picture of war; the trainload of fresh men gliding proudly up the line, the ruined men sliding slowly down, and all the while the guns in the open trucks making one's heart leap as guns always do, and reviving that pernicious feeling, so difficult to get rid of, that war is glorious after all. (chap. 12)

The lyricism of this passage, in which, characteristically, pacifistic dissent rises briefly to check the note of heroism, represents one end of an experiential spectrum whose other extreme is demonstrated by remarks related to Orwell's time in the trenches a few months before. Speaking of the endless search for firewood, Orwell remarks with dry economy: "The point about the firewood was that there was practically no firewood to be had" (chap. 3); and of rough-and-ready attempts to keep warm by standing in red-hot embers: "It was bad for your boots but it was very good for your feet" (chap.4). His time in Spain was a decisive turning point for Orwell as a politically conscious human being; concomitantly, the book he wrote about it displays more consistently than hitherto that clarity and simplicity of style we now call "Orwellian," whether he is presenting in vigorous, suspenseful, and unsentimental detail a night attack in which he and other volunteers temporarily captured a Fascist redoubt (chap. 7), or describing the three days he spent in the roof of the Poliorama cinema in Barcelona in the imminent expectation that P.O.U.M. headquarters opposite would be attacked by Civil Guards—"a sort of violent inertia, a nightmare of noise without movement" (chap. 10).

In comparison with the irritation and confusion that often thicken his prose in part 2 of *The Road to Wigan Pier,* Orwell's writing in *Homage to Catalonia* displays not only a warm and eloquent involvement but an ironic, sometimes humorous detachment. Commenting on being shot by a sniper, Orwell remarks that "the whole experience of being hit by a bullet is very interesting, and I think it is worth describing in detail" (chap. 12). Physically he felt no pain, instead a sensation like an electric shock; emotionally he resented the thought of death rather than feared it. A similar refusal to embellish facts or parade responses marks his comments on the mass arrests of P.O.U.M. members, which were kept secret from P.O.U.M. front-line troops: "This kind of thing is a little difficult to forgive" (chap. 13). The most he permits himself to say about the arrest of Georges Kopp, his battalion commander, which spurred him to make a brave but unsuccessful attempt to intervene, is, "I admit I was angry when I heard of Kopp's arrest." The mixture here of patient restraint and Swiftian deadly understatement may well have been intended to serve both a long-term and a short-term purpose. While recognizably embodying for posterity his disillusion with left-wing ingratitude, it avoided alienating those who, in the Spain of 1938, might have read his book and responded to the concern of one who, whatever his sectional loyalties, had fought on the government side, and thus deserved to be listened to.

The atmosphere of Orwell's last two chapters, describing these dismaying events and his own few days as a fugitive from the purge—dining in expensive restaurants by day as protective camouflage, and by night scrawling "Visca P.O.U.M.!" on their walls and sleeping out in a gutted church—is a complex and forceful blend of absurdity, fear, resilience, "a deep desire for this damned nonsense [the pursuit] to be over" (chap. 13), and, over the French border in Banyuls, a wish that "we [Orwell's wife had been with him in Barcelona] had stayed to be imprisoned along with the others" (chap. 14). In the book's final paragraphs, describing Orwell's arrival first in Paris, "gay and prosperous . . . after poor Spain," then in England, "probably the sleekest landscape in the world," relief and regret are inextricably mingled.

When *Homage to Catalonia* was published—after the seven months of writing that followed Orwell's return to Wallington, and just a few days before Franco's forces drove a wedge to the sea between Catalonia and the southern portion of the shrunken republic in Valencia—response to it was based more on varying attitudes to its political raw material than on perception of the power of its writing and the poignancy with which it gave permanence to a short-lived flowering of human aspiration. This contemporary reaction was not surprising, and in a letter to Cyril Connolly Orwell noted "better reviews than I had expected."[28] With the passage of time, however, and the vanishing of its events into history, the book's stature as the finest of Orwell's nonfictional longer works, and indeed as one of his best works, is clear. At the end of his penultimate chapter of his history of the Spanish Civil War, Hugh Thomas has stated that "the few real masterpieces that were produced [in that period] will survive as monuments to those who died."[29] Among these "few real masterpieces" are W. H. Auden's "Spain," Stephen Spender's "Two Armies," and Ernest Hemingway's *For Whom the Bell Tolls*. *Homage to Catalonia* is also of that number.

Chapter Five

Orwell the Essayist

In January 1939, having just finished the rough draft of *Coming Up for Air,* Orwell mentioned in a letter to Geoffrey Gorer "an idea for a very big novel, in fact 3 in series, making something about the size of *War and Peace.*"[1] He wryly acknowledged that "projecting a Saga" might be "a sign of approaching senile decay"; but added that "in my case it may merely be another way of saying that I hope war won't break out, because I don't think I could write a Saga in the middle of a war." The Second World War broke out seven months later; nevertheless, in a note on himself supplied for a reference book in April 1940, Orwell referred more definitely to his idea now as "a long novel in three parts, to be called either *The Lion and the Unicorn* or *The Quick and the Dead.*" Its first part he hoped to produce "by some time in 1941."[2] No novel of either name by Orwell ever appeared, nor did he later refer to it. But since the total abandonment of a notion once mentioned to others was uncharacteristic of Orwell, one is tempted to agree with Bernard Crick, who on the evidence of some manuscript pages headed "For 'The Quick and the Dead'" has speculated that Orwell's projected "family saga" trilogy did in fact get partly written,[3] and consisted of *Nineteen Eighty-Four* as its culmination, and *Animal Farm* (though in a different mode) as its intermediate episode. It lacked only its first volume, which, if written, might have dealt with the childhood of Winston Smith's father.[4] Such a hypothesis, Crick points out, adds force to Orwell's original title for *Nineteen Eighty-Four,* "The Last Man in Europe"; it may also help to explain why that resonant title remained unused.

Whatever happened to Orwell's idea for a long novel, he did not discard one of its intended titles, "The Lion and the Unicorn." Instead, he attached it to the longest of his essays, added the subtitle "Socialism and the English Genius," retained the three-part structure envisaged for the novel, and published the result as a separate book of some sixty pages in 1941. The essay/book was his most extended treatment of the power of nationalism in the contemporary world, the nature of the English character and the English middle classes, and the possibility that, in wartime, England might be transformed from a place "haunted by the idea of human equality" into a revolutionary country able to put that idea into practice and thus remain true to its deepest self.[5] *The Lion and the Unicorn* turned the lessons Orwell had learned in northern England and in republican Spain into a message aimed at all his compatriots, and established Orwell as one of the most lucid, sane, and eloquent voices in a decade of upheaval and change, equally concerned to preserve the best of the past and, while warning his readers of the forces that menaced it, to argue for a humane and decent future. Whereas his two remaining novels of the 1940s, *Animal Farm* and *Nineteen Eighty-Four,* imaginatively focus his doubts and his pessimism, his many essays and pieces of journalism during the same decade convey discursively a far wider range of observation and comment on life and literature, whose total effect bears witness to a lively resilience.

In April 1946, a year after World War II ended, Orwell reestablished contact with his former Eton tutor, A. S. F. Gow, and described how moving from Wallington to London in May 1940 had altered the pattern of his literary life, bringing a mixture of advantages and disadvantages: "The last few years life has been so ghastly expensive that I find the only way I can write books is to write long essays for the magazines and then reprint them. However all this hack work I have done in the last few years has had the advantage that it gets me a new public, and when I do publish a book it sells a lot more than mine used to before the war."[6] Orwell's letter was written just two months after the appearance of *Critical Essays,* which brought together ten pieces originally published between 1939 and 1945. These, though, and the longer essays collected in *Inside the Whale* in 1940, were only the impressive tip of an iceberg of journalism produced by Orwell during the war years and after, a little more of which, together with two prewar essays, was to thrust into collective visibility in the posthumously published *Shooting an Elephant* in 1950.

What Orwell modestly described to Gow as "hack work" had taken two main forms. From 1941 to 1943 Orwell was employed as a Talks Producer with the British Broadcasting Corporation, in charge of programs beamed out to India and Southeast Asia. Many of these broadcast talks, often on literary topics, he wrote himself; their clear style and carefully paced unfolding of an argument, as for instance in "Tolstoy and Shakespeare" (1941) and "The Rediscovery of Europe" (1942), show how well Orwell could adapt to a new medium.[7] At the same time, however, he supplied many long "London Letters" to the American magazine *Partisan Review,* concerning himself with the progress of the war and the political shifts that accompanied it. These long essays continued until the summer of 1946, and overlapped with new responsibilities Orwell took on after resigning from the BBC. In 1943 he became Literary Editor of the left-wing weekly *Tribune,* one of whose editorial directors was Aneurin Bevan, "the one politician whom Orwell thoroughly respected."[8] This was an even more active job, and more congenial, than the quasi-official BBC; as well as vetting the material submitted by others, often as softheartedly as his own creation Ravelston in *Keep the Aspidistra Flying,* Orwell contributed his own regular column entitled "As I Please," which lasted until 1947, a year longer than he kept the editorship. Bernard Crick has calculated that Orwell wrote no fewer than seventy-one of his plain-speaking, free-ranging editorial articles in a period of little over three years. But even this was not all. Throughout the decade Orwell wrote for a wide spectrum of other newspapers and magazines, from *Horizon,* edited by his Eton friend Cyril Connolly, to the *Contemporary Jewish Record* (an article of 1945 on "Anti-semitism in Britain"), and the magazine *Polemic,* in which among other things he published the last of his major literary essays, "Lear, Tolstoy and the Fool" (1947). Orwell's staggering rate of productivity may be summed up by reference to a single year: in 1944, in addition to writing three important essays, including the nostalgic "Raffles and Miss Blandish," he contributed 110 "reviews or short articles" to *Tribune,* the *Observer,* and the *Manchester Evening News,* for which he wrote a weekly book column from December 1943 until November 1946.[9]

Three of the four volumes in Orwell's *Collected Essays, Journalism and Letters,* published by Secker and Warburg in 1968, are devoted to his work of the 1940s; only one to the previous two decades. Clearly Orwell was accurate in telling Gow that his "hack work" had brought him "a new public," and despite the increasing republication in recent years of his four prewar novels and his three prewar nonfictional books, it seems likely that Orwell is still best known to many as the author of *Animal Farm* and *Nineteen Eighty-Four,* and as a writer of essays. A number of these resemble Orwell's two most famous novels in that they attempt to fulfill the ambition he had formed in 1936 and declared in his essay "Why I Write" ten years later: "to make political writing into an art."[10] One thinks here of such essays as "Notes on Nationalism" (1945) and "The Prevention of Literature" (1946), where the combination of clear statement with widely relevant and highly contemporary subject matter suggests that, after the confused impulses of his prewar novels, Orwell had found not only his true voice but the ideal new form in which to use it.

But two points in modification of this view need to be made. Not all, not even a majority, of Orwell's essays can usefully be classified as political. Many are analyses and appreciations of writers he admired, cultural phenomena he enjoyed, experiences that delighted or haunted him; they are full of interest for the reader, since Orwell was a quirky and intelligent observer, but their author's deepest impulse in writing them is to preserve. Moreover, the essay form itself was old-fashioned, having enjoyed its heyday in the first three decades of Orwell's life. That no writer since Orwell has employed it so frequently or with such distinction makes his use of it, however personally accented, one of the last fine flowerings of a mode of writing favored by "men of letters" and directed at an educated, but not specialist, audience.

Of the many pieces Orwell wrote, mostly from 1939 onwards, and mostly for newspapers and literary magazines, only eleven were published in his lifetime in collections. Three long essays appeared in *Inside the Whale* (1940); two of these were republished, with eight shorter ones added, in *Critical Essays* (1946). It was only after Orwell's death that his essays began to reappear in large numbers. They did so in diverse separate and often reprinted packagings, from *Shooting an Elephant* (Secker and Warburg, 1950) to *Decline of the English Murder* (Penguin Books, 1965), which taken together give the impression, if not precisely of a posthumously exploited reputation, then of a cautious, rationed dispensation, like that of diamonds issued on the market in timed batches to keep the price up. "Posthumous sweepings seldom cohere," said E. M. Forster tartly in his review of *Shooting an Elephant,*[11] and it must be admitted that, though this and later collections seldom overlap each others' "territory," the internal variety in each leads to a collective impression of randomness and confusion. There is no organization either along thematic lines or in the chronological order that Orwell himself adopted in *Critical Essays.* The impression of randomness is compounded by the publishers' failure to distinguish (or explicitly to set aside any distinction between) different types of "essay." Orwell himself reprinted none of his pieces from *Tribune*; *Shooting an Elephant,* however, reprinted nine of them. *England Your England* (Secker and Warburg, 1953) included part 1, only, of *The Lion and the Unicorn*; and also, at some distance from each other, two chapters from *The Road to Wigan Pier,* under the titles "North and South" and "Down the Mine."[12] The latter essay reappeared in the Penguin *Selected Essays* of 1957, whose title was confusingly changed to *Inside the Whale* when the selection was reprinted in 1962.

The recent publication, in 1984, of *The Penguin Essays of George Orwell* has put a convenient end to this bibliographers' nightmare by bringing together forty-one pieces in all, dating from 1931 to 1949, and arranging them in chronological order. There is a single exception to this: as in the four-volume *Collected Essays, Journalism and Letters* (1968) from which many of the pieces are taken, Orwell's "Why I Write" is printed first, an exercise that immediately thrusts on the reader an attitude to Orwell's work that he himself reached, or at any rate expressed, only after half his essays, and considerably more than half his work, had been written. There is, clearly, still an irritating element of quasi-official "packaging" in the presentation of Orwell's work.

The Penguin collection is by no means complete. It omits, among other things, prose pieces unpublished in Orwell's lifetime, like "Hop-Picking" (1931) and "Clink" (1932), which Orwell made use of in *A Clergyman's Daughter* and *Keep the Aspidistra Flying*; but since "The Spike" (*Adelphi* 1931), which it includes, was also adapted in *Down and Out in Paris and London,* the omission of the other pieces seems arbitrary. And Orwell's better-known literary essays, on Dickens, Swift, Kipling, P. G. Wodehouse and Arthur Koestler, could have been augmented by the inclusion of his essays on Charles Reade (*New Statesman* 1940) and Tobias Smollett (*Tribune* 1944), together with his essay on George Gissing (1948), which did not see print until 1960. Leaving aside many of Orwell's "As I Please" columns for *Tribune,* which are justifiably omitted since their treatment of any single subject is very brief, there are approaching twenty pieces in the four-volume compilation that could have been added to those in the Penguin collection of 1984. Nevertheless, it is by far the most comprehensive volume of Orwell's essays available, not only providing more than enough material for comment, but by its sensible chronological presentation (the position of "Why I Write" excepted) allowing a sense of Orwell's development as a writer of essays to emerge.

In bringing together within one set of covers a substantial number of Orwell's essays—two-thirds, say, of the eligible material currently available in published form—the Penguin volume also simplifies the task of classification: a necessary task where material is too large and diverse for comment on all of it to be possible, or for detailed sampling of a few items to be fair to the silently excluded remainder. Only a rough taxonomy is possible, since some essays slide between categories; but it can at least indicate recurrent types of subject and approach, as well as show what sorts of topic interested Orwell when.

There are approximately five discernible groupings in Orwell's essays, together with two essays that illustrate interests not pursued by Orwell anywhere else. These two are "Marrakech" (1939), his only prose piece primarily concerned to convey the atmosphere of a place; and "Reflections on Gandhi" (1949), his last completed essay, and his only one devoted to a person—a public figure, that is, rather than one whose human interest derives incidentally from his art. Both essays touch on political matters—French and British colonialism respectively, and their accompanying exploitation of one skin color by another—but their essential emphases are, in the five-page "Marrakech," local color, and in "Reflections on Gandhi" a wish to tease out the various elements in an individual whose "sainthood" irritated Orwell but also, toward the end of his own life, intrigued him. Both essays may be considered accidents, "Marrakech" resulting from Orwell's stay in Morocco for force majeure reasons of health, "Reflections on Gandhi" (published not in England but in America) having probably been prompted by Gandhi's assassination in 1948—though its concern with the respective claims of humanism and otherworldliness links it with "Politics vs. Literature" (1946) and "Lear, Tolstoy and the Fool" (1947). The dates of the two essays bracket Orwell's most productive period as a writer of discursive prose, and serve to point up the rarity in it of an interest in geographical and psychological specifics, in unique particulars rather than factors capable of general human application.

Orwell's few early essays, published between 1931 and 1936, together with a minority of those he wrote in the next decade, derived either from the life-style of his formative years at school and in Burma, or from the experiences he later sought out to counteract them in Paris and London. If one excludes "Looking Back on the Spanish War" (1943) as having an essentially historicopolitical emphasis (its ragbag nature makes it, in any case, less an essay than an addition to *Homage to Catalonia*), there are six essays of this type, from "The Spike" (1931) to "Such, Such Were the Joys," completed in 1947. All, because of their source in Orwell's personal experience, can simply be classified as "autobiographical"; but there is a difference between them, exemplified by the two mentioned. Whereas the second deals at considerable length, and with much subjective elaboration, with an experience itself lengthy and traumatic, the first is concentrated around a single, brief situation, and presents it as objectively as possible: one is aware of Orwell as an observing eye but not to any great extent as a commentator, much less a reformer. "The Spike" narrows the autobiographical essay down to the transcription of an "event"; a category useful for describing "A Hanging" (1931), with its poignant but unelaborated juxtaposition of life and death, and to a lesser extent "Shooting an Elephant" (1936), where an antiimperial slant is educed from a dilemma that its protagonist nevertheless admits he could have resolved differently. "Bookshop Memories" (1936), by comparison, is merely a loose set of reminiscences; and "How the Poor Die" (1946),[13] for all the starkness of its picture of Paris hospital conditions (a 1929 nightmare of death among strangers, perhaps recalled by Orwell's increasingly bad health seventeen years later), has behind it a Proustian attempt to track the sense of déjà vu those conditions gave him to its source in Orwell's memory of hearing Tennyson's poem "The Children's Hospital" read aloud when he was six. It can thus be said to span not "several weeks" of Orwell's life, but forty years.

"A Hanging" is probably Orwell's most celebrated essay of the 1930s. Hardly more than a sketch, but packed with sharply observed detail, it is stark and haunting at once. It displays, however, a detachment and tentativeness that are uncharacteristic of Orwell's essays as a whole and that largely vanished from them by the end of the decade, when he had gained a literary reputation and the sense of an audience "out there" that he could address directly,. Even in "Shooting an Elephant" these powers of unopinionated recording, particularly evident, for instance, when Orwell describes the elephant's slow death agonies, were starting to be overlaid by a wish to make points: the incident is offered less for itself than as a paradigm of imperial uneasiness. By 1939, too, the essay of autobiography and "event" had itself largely been displaced by the three categories of essay by which Orwell is most particularly identified: essays concerned with popular culture, beginning with "Boys' Weeklies" (1940); essays devoted to art and letters, most often to a particular writer, beginning with "Charles Dickens" (1939); and essays, beginning with "My Country Right or Left" (1940), that can broadly be called "political," though in them, on the whole, questions of ideology are mixed with, or subordinated to, a concern with Englishness, history, language, censorship, and the writer's place in an increasingly monolithic system. The air of most of these essays, that of "a man speaking to men," in the confidence that reason must surely prevail, or at least obtain a fair hearing, conveys a mind both independent in its judgments and yet conscious of having many interests in common with others. Orwell voice in peacetime had often sounded private, and many of his experiences had been remote, solitary, even alienated; in wartime London he was at the center of events, and his voice took on, without hollowness, a public tone.

Nostalgia, natural as one response to the onset of war, and already revealed in *Coming Up for Air,* is the keynote of a number of Orwell's essays, at least up to 1946, and particularly of his three essays, of diminishing length, on aspects of popular culture, a subject whose close study Orwell was among the first to pioneer.[14] The essays are "Boys' Weeklies," "The Art of Donald McGill" (1942), and "Decline of the English Murder" (1946); to which may be added his two-page piece in *Tribune* entitled "In Defence of English Cooking" (1945).

The ostensible thrust of "Boys' Weeklies" emerges at the end, in Orwell's remark that "popular imaginative literature is a field that left-wing thought has never begun to enter,"[15] and in his view that it should attempt to do so, and thus increase the contemporary relevance of writing for young people. But this is only after a long discussion of the characters, motifs, and assumptions of the magazines read by schoolboys, from the old *Gem* and *Magnet* to the new *Wizard* and *Hotspur,* that is so independently engrossing that it is hard to escape the conclusion that Orwell's subtext is a far from critical harking-back to a past in which "everything is solid, safe and unquestionable. Everything will be the same for ever and ever" (96). The world of Billy Bunter's Greyfriars School was an upper-class one, and its assumptions essentially imperialist; but Orwell's enjoyment extended also to the working-class phenomenon of the comic postcard, an old-fashioned enclave of sexual innuendo, hen-pecked husbands, and fat-bottomed wives. For Orwell, the comic postcard was simultaneously a safety valve for ignoble impulses, a raspberry blown at high official ideals, and yet, fundamentally, an upholder of the natural progression from youth to age, of which the institution of marriage was the embodiment. Orwell himself possessed a sizeable collection of "The Art of Donald McGill" (the supreme postcard artist);[16] his essay is a masterly development from vulgar details to his final generalization that comic postcards represent an element, once part of "the central stream of literature," that has descended to "a barely legal existence in cheap stationers' windows" (209). "I for one should be sorry to see them vanish," Orwell concluded, more unequivocal about a proletarian form of expression than he had been about the dream empire of the private school. What was actually vanishing was regretfully noted in his short essay "Decline of the English Murder"—the kind of murder (staple prewar newspaper reading after the traditional Sunday lunch Orwell himself enjoyed) that had been committed "after long and terrible wrestles with his conscience," and with "strong emotions," by an "intensely respectable man" for serious reasons. Such a murder, the product of an "all-prevailing hypocrisy" of "a stable society," had been replaced by mere meaningless violence with "no depth of feeling in it": the callous so-called "Cleft Chin murder," three in fact, committed for trivial gain by a couple, one of them American, who were together for only a few days. Clearly Orwell's essay does not advocate murder of any kind; beneath the illustrative sermon his text is the loss of order brought about by the war and by what he saw as a dilution of English values by various kinds of transatlantic influence. If the latter view was narrow-minded, it was nevertheless shared by many of Orwell's compatriots at this time.

A similar kind of regret for the decline in moral attitudes is conveyed by Orwell's essay of 1944, "Raffles and Miss Blandish," which contrasts the sadistic violence of James Hadley Chase's novel *No Orchids for Miss Blandish* (1939), set in America and very popular in England "during the Battle of Britain and the Blitz" (266), with the infinitely milder wickedness recorded by E. W. Hornung at the turn of the century in his books about Raffles, the upper-class "amateur cracksman" whose life of crime still had wafting through it the remembered code of "the public school man," for whom certain things, like robbing one's host, were simply "not done." Orwell's nostalgic affection for Raffles, who still had some standards of behavior, is very apparent; the world of *No Orchids,* sexually sophisticated and totally amoral, is deeply repugnant to him, reflecting a "might is right" principle that he finds indistinguishable from fascism—a subject he had touched on in 1943 in his short essay on W. B. Yeats.

These two essays belong to the "literary" category of Orwell's prose pieces, which spanned the years 1939 to 1947 and beyond (if one counts Orwell's plans, in 1949, for essays on Joseph Conrad and Evelyn Waugh). The category is much the largest of the five, consisting of some fifteen pieces. It is also, partly because of its size, the one that involves the greatest degree of overlap with others, since Orwell's tastes in, or awareness of, literature ranged from highbrow (Yeats, Arthur

Koestler) through middlebrow (Kipling, Leonard Merrick's *Helen's Babies,* celebrated in "Riding Down from Bangor" [1946]) to lowbrow (*No Orchids*); literature and life, for him, not being separable, his essays centered on writers and writing reach out frequently to touch on popular culture and contemporary politics, and in one instance ("Books v. Cigarettes" [1946]) household economics. They also come at their subjects from varying angles and convey a variety of subtexts: though with many acute things to say about individual authors, Orwell rarely treats their work in the precise, technical manner of an academic scholar/critic. The "plain man" character of his approach is captured by a remark in "Lear, Tolstoy and the Fool" that would surely have set him beyond the pale for such a stern assessor of comparative excellence as F. R. Leavis: "In reality there is no kind of evidence or argument by which one can show that Shakespeare, or any other writer, is 'good'. Nor is there any way of definitely proving that—for instance—Warwick Deeping is 'bad'. Ultimately there is no test for literary merit except survival, which is itself merely an index to majority opinion" (410).

"Charles Dickens," the earliest (1939) and by far the longest of Orwell's literary essays, uses close examination of texts and characters not only to express a long-standing delight in Dicken's "rococo . . . fertility of invention," but to argue a convincing case that Dickens, however "subversive" in his attacks on many English institutions, was neither a proletarian nor a revolutionary writer. Essentially, in Orwell's view, he was a bourgeois moralist, conditioned by his background and experiences, who offered no political remedies for social ills, only the notion, "not such a platitude as it sounds," that "if men would behave decently the world would be decent" (54). Though richly grounded in a knowledge of Dickens's novels (Orwell shrewdly, and without hostility, notes Dickens's lack of emphasis on work and his ideal of a life in which "nothing ever happens, except the yearly childbirth" [73]), the essay is something of an unconscious self-portrait, especially when it selects as Dickens's most salient characteristic "a hatred of tyranny" and admires his work as the expression of "the native decency of the common man." What clearly appealed to Orwell as a mid-twentieth-century reader of Dickens was his old-fashioned liberal independent-mindedness, so welcome a corrective to what Orwell dismissively called "the smelly little orthodoxies which are now contending for our souls."

Orwell's admiration for Dickens was wholehearted, as was his admiration for Shakespeare, whose noble, struggling humanism and "interest in the actual processes of life" (413) he championed eloquently, eight years later, in "Lear, Tolstoy and the Fool," against what he saw as Tolstoy's Christian, but intolerant, impatience with the things of this world. In both cases he was defending writers he loved against the attacks and misconceptions of others—as in 1945 he also, out of a mixture of literary enjoyment and chivalrous decency, defended P. G. Wodehouse against continuing hostility to his "collaboration" with the Nazis, allegedly manifested in a few naive broadcasts from Berlin in 1941. Between these two major essays, however, Orwell wrote of writers and artists whom he admired less completely, but to whose good qualities and artistic merits he wished, equally strongly, to be fair: Rudyard Kipling, Salvador Dali, and Jonathan Swift.

Orwell's enjoyment of Kipling may have proceeded partly from fellow feeling: much of the latter's development, Orwell writes,"is traceable to his having been born in India and having left school early." Certainly, in spite of an initial admission that Kipling was "a jingo imperialist . . . morally insensitive and aesthetically disgusting," most of Orwell's essay, published in 1942, conveys an admiration that, as in "Boys' Weeklies," undercuts criticism and is surely associated with Orwell's own memories of the British colonial East, with whose "official class" Kipling identified yet for whose rank-and-file soldiery he was the eloquent popular voice. Part of Orwell's admiration indicated his own uncertain position between a liberalism he felt bound to support and a conservative nostalgia he could not repress. He praises Kipling for "a sense of responsibility" when confronting the practical operations of empire: this gave him an unhypocritical honesty beyond the reach of the idealistic class that in "My Country Right or Left" (1940) Orwell had dismissed in the phrase "the boiled rabbits of the Left" (144). Whatever his failings as a thinker, Kipling as a poet possessed the cardinal virtue of memorability, being able time after time to hit off "some emotion which nearly every human being can share." To this far from negligible talent Orwell applied the term "good bad poetry,"[17] whose existence was for him a "sign of the emotional overlap between the intellectual and the ordinary man."

He found no such artistic quality in the paintings, and more particularly the exhibitionistic autobiography, of Salvador Dali, whom he dealt with two years later in his essay "Benefit of Clergy" (1944). For Orwell, Dali was an "undesirable human being" and "as antisocial as a flea" (257), and he saw no virtue in any approach to art that would argue that the artist was exempt, by reason of his skill, from the ordinary moral judgments of society. Neither, however (and the true point of the essay, which verges on the political, lies here), could Orwell accept the extreme opposite view: that art itself should be judged by a moral yardstick. Such a "highbrow-baiting" attitude was "dangerous," dismissive not only of Dali's painting but of the writings of Joyce, Proust, D. H. Lawrence, and T. S. Eliot. For Orwell the correct response was clear-cut: Dali was an "atrocious" egoist with a "diseased" imagination, but also "a draughtsman of very exceptional gifts." It is an ironic comment on Orwell's wish to be accurate about Dali that his fair-minded and well-documented essay was suppressed by his publishers on the grounds of obscenity, when the book in which it was to appear was in the final stages of printing.[18]

Orwell's interest in Swift centered on *Gulliver's Travels,* which he discussed very perceptively in his essay of 1946, "Politics vs. Literature." Whereas Orwell's hostility to Dali's personality was set against a fair-minded but rather theoretical wish to do justice to his skill as a painter, with Swift Orwell was in a more evenly balanced quandary, hence his title, which expresses briefly what Orwell restates fully towards the end of the essay: "What is the relationship between agreement with a writer's opinions, and the enjoyment of his work?" (390). As some of Dali's pictures were "diseased," so Swift "is a diseased writer," permanently depressed, disgusted with the body, unable to "believe that life . . . could be made worth living," perversely hostile to science, and (insofar as the picture of the Houyhnhnms reflects Swift's own views) attracted not, admittedly, by enforced government control but by its even more dangerous later stage: an orthodoxy of feeling and opinion so ingrained in society that disagreement seems merely absurd. For Orwell, Swift's volatile rebelliousness was in no way left-wing, but represented a Tory anarchism that "despised authority while disbelieving in liberty." All in all, Swift's "world view . . . only just passes the test of sanity." Yet Orwell had to reconcile this with his own lifelong, often renewed enjoyment of *Gulliver's Travels,* which he calls "a great work of art." He did so by pointing to Swift's "terrible intensity of vision," which was able to compel the reader's temporary acceptance of a partial view of life: everyone had Swift's negative feelings "at least intermittently" (391). It was not so much that Swift invented what was not true, as that he omitted from the record much that was. But however irresistible Orwell found Swift as an imaginative writer, he found his attitudes as unpalatable as those of Tolstoy, discussed more fully the following year (1947) in "Lear, Tolstoy and the Fool." Like Tolstoy, Swift disbelieved in "the possibility of happiness," a matter upon which, for Orwell, "all serious political controversy really turns" (386), and which he himself was touching on at that time, though not hopefully, in *Nineteen Eighty-Four.*

The possibility of happiness does not figure greatly, per se, in the fifth, "political," category of Orwell's essays, which number no more than ten—some of them, like "Inside the Whale" (1940), considerably overlapping on the "literary" category. Where happiness occurs, Orwell believes, it is usually in defiance of politics, as indicated by two pieces published in 1946 in *Tribune,* "Some Thoughts on the Common Toad" and "A Good Word for the Vicar of Bray." Both essays, "lightweight" at first glance and delightful to read, press the claims of the ever-renewed physical world as against the opinionated operations of the time-bound human mind. Notorious for his turncoat allegiances, the Vicar of Bray (a village on the Thames a few miles from Eton) nevertheless did the future a service by planting what turned into a magnificent yew tree, just as Orwell, by planting at Wallington rose bushes and Cox's Orange Pippin apples ("a good fruit to be known by"), had added visual and edible pleasure to the world without consciously intending to. "Some Thoughts on the Common Toad" adopts a more lyrical tone to celebrate the pleasures of spring, which cost nothing and exist totally outside the control of disapproving bureaucrats. More profoundly, they represent just that sort of innocent enjoyment at which schemes of political amelioration ought to aim and so often do not. If Orwell had abandoned poetry in the late 1930s "to make political writing into an art," as he stated in the same year in "Why I Write" (1946), he had not forgotten the impulse behind it, asserting the relevance of his nonpolitical observations memorably thus: "If man cannot enjoy the return of Spring, why should he be happy in a labour-saving Utopia?" (368).

But the "Utopia" is a rhetorical figment. No utopias are suggested by Orwell's political essays during the war years, or after; except for an initial hope expressed in the long patriotic essay *The Lion and the Unicorn,* written at the start of the war as, to quote its attention-getting opening, "highly civilized human beings are flying overhead, trying to kill me" (144). Orwell's focus was on England, "a family with the wrong members in control"—an outmoded ruling class that, he hoped, would be replaced by a more egalitarian system. Like the Spanish Anarchists (whose view had not prevailed), Orwell saw the necessary war against Hitler as properly accompanied by a domestic revolution, out of which would emerge an England more democratic and thus more "true to herself." This optimistic note, however, is undercut by two essays of 1945. The first, "Anti-Semitism in Britain," describes anti-Semitism as one form of a larger problem, the "disease loosely called nationalism" (292). The second, "Notes on Nationalism," written four months later, carefully distinguishes nationalism, which is "inseparable from the desire for power" (306), from patriotism, which is essentially defensive—"devotion to a particular place and a particular way of life." The difficulty with nationalism (of which communism was one variety) was that its protean range of forms made it hard to recognize clearly, let alone combat.

Orwell's identifications of them in his essay, of course, were one form of combat: that of an intelligent, responsible, and honest person who happened to be a writer. His clarity of vision not only isolated the problems of his own day and placed them permanently in the historical record, but also, by showing their origin in uncivilized instincts of the human heart, points later readers to their recurrence and acts as a warning. Because of this, it is hard to imagine Orwell's political comments ever ceasing to have some relevance. A similar form of contemporary combat, Orwell's famous essay "Politics and the English Language" (1946), seems likely to have had an effect in his own time, since some of the clichés of political speech at which it jeers—"Achilles Heel," "melting pot," "acid test" (366)—seem virtually to have vanished, at least in Great Britain. But Orwell's essay does the even more valuable service of noting the dangerous downward spiral whereby muddled thought leads to unclear language and unclear language furthers increasing vagueness of thought, a vagueness exploited by officials and regimes for ends far worse than the debasement of language. The derision of a literate person at more recent formulations like "on-going counter-productive situation" may owe something to Orwell's satirical attack on the shoddy phraseology of the 1940s; more important, one is made aware how euphemistic jargon ("let go" for "dismiss," for instance), or pseudoscientific precision ("defoliation"), can be a cloak for inhumane actions.

"The process is reversible," Orwell remarked in 1946 of the decline of language (355), and his essay made its contribution, fighting against the current, to reverse it. Language, however, is used for imaginative purposes, for creating a fictional world as well as for describing an observed one. Though a writer of much discursive prose during the

1940s, as commentator, preserver, and critic, Orwell had up to 1939 been a novelist. Three of his essays, spanning the years 1940 to 1948, reiterate a view of the writer's dilemma that makes it clear how difficult continuing to be a novelist had become, and the one in which that view is first expressed, "Inside the Whale" (1940), jibes oddly with the confidence shown the same year at the end of *The Lion and the Unicorn.* All three essays (the others are "The Prevention of Literature" [1946] and "Writers and Leviathan" [1948]) could be called either literary or political, pivoting as they do on the writer's position in an increasingly totalitarian world.

Like the "Leviathan" of Thomas Hobbes, referred to in the title of Orwell's 1948 essay, the "whale" of Orwell's essay of 1940 is the state, or the historical process, which embraces or swallows the individual, a fate that, according to temperament, may be comforting, fearsome, or neutral. The notion of being "inside" the whale was derived from a remark made by the expatriate American writer Henry Miller, whose novel *Tropic of Cancer* had so impressed Orwell that he devoted one of his longest essays partly to recommending it and putting its alleged "obscenity" into perspective, but mostly to placing it in the context of twentieth-century literary attitudes and thus to indicating the unusual nature of Miller's response to the worsening political situation of the 1930s. On his way to Barcelona late in 1936, Orwell had met Henry Miller in Paris and been struck by his total detachment from the Spanish Civil War and the challenge it represented for Orwell. Strangely perhaps, Orwell was not repelled by Miller's apolitical stance, and similarly was not repelled by Miller's novel, set in the lost world of drifters and artists in the Paris Orwell himself had experienced in the late 1920s. Totally unlike the political writers of the 1930s (whom Orwell surveys, together with the writers of the two previous decades, in the long, literary central section of his essay), Miller eschewed in his novel any "serious purpose," and instead conveyed a note of happiness and "acceptance," of pleasant and unpleasant phenomena alike. Like Jonah, Miller was "inside the whale"; but this did not blind him to the state of the world, simply he did not "feel called on to do anything about it" (132).

If it was accompanied, as in *Tropic of Cancer,* by "emotional sincerity" and lack of fear, such a passive response seemed to Orwell the only one likely to ensure a good novel in "an age of totalitarian dictatorships . . . in which freedom of thought will be at first a deadly sin and later a meaningless abstraction" (137). The writer, "liberal" by definition, could take no part "as a writer" in the evolution of the new, unfree society; all he or she could do was "accept it, endure it, record it," and by so doing express an attitude close to the experience of the ordinary person, something Orwell had tried to do, somewhat clumsily, in the final section of *Coming Up for Air.* By the time he wrote "The Prevention of Literature," the likelihood of any individual response to experience by the writer seemed to have diminished: "the autonomous individual" was more and more pressured by political orthodoxy and various forms of government control, and "literature is doomed if liberty of thought perishes" (346). The penultimate essay Orwell wrote, "Writers and Leviathan," assumes as axiomatic a world in which "War, Fascism, concentration camps, rubber truncheons, atomic bombs . . . are what we daily think about" (459). The "compunction" engendered by such a world had made "a purely aesthetic attitude towards life . . . impossible"; and yet "acceptance of *any* political discipline seems to be incompatible with literary integrity" (462–63). For Orwell, the writer's position had become virtually unworkable, stranded between a humanly impossible detachment and an artistically destructive involvement. All that was left for a conscientious human being was to choose the lesser of two evils, and then to act; all that the human being could do and still be a writer was to keep part of the self "inviolate," the "saner self that stands aside, records the things that are done and admits their necessity, but refuses to be deceived as to their true nature" (464–65).

In his two fictional works of the 1940s, *Animal Farm* and *Nineteen Eighty-Four,* Orwell did a little better than this. Although, refusing to be deceived, he recorded what had been done and stated a warning about what might be done, he could not bring himself to admit its necessity. This, one may say, was the side of Orwell that, against the pressures of the times, yet aware of them, was still able to express itself in creative writing. But Orwell could no longer confront the world directly. Unable to emulate the "acceptance" he had approved in Henry Miller, he was also unable to set his last fictions in a totally recognizable contemporary world. In order to deal with the Leviathan of the totalitarian state yet preserve his imaginative freedom, he turned away from the sort of novel he had written before the war: first to an allegorical fable of the recent past, then, finally, to a vision of a dystopian future.

Chapter Six
Animal Farm

In his essay on Arthur Koestler (1944) Orwell points out how rare it is to find, in English writing, anything "of aesthetic value" that can be compared with Ignazio Silone's *Fontamara* (1934) and Koestler's own *Darkness at Noon* (1940), novels that belong to "the special class of literature that has arisen out of the European political struggle since the rise of Fascism."[1] More particularly, since almost no English writers had experience of totalitarianism, he notes that "there exists in England almost no literature of disillusionment with the Soviet Union." Instead, that country is viewed either with "ignorant disapproval" or with "uncritical admiration."

Some months before his essay on Koestler, however, Orwell had completed his own memorable contribution to that "literature of disillusion," his novella *Animal Farm,* which he had written immediately after resigning from the BBC in November 1943 and becoming literary editor of *Tribune.* His job at *Tribune* took up only three days a week, and he finished *Animal Farm* in the short space of four months, in February 1944. Just before finishing it, he described it to a friend, with coy evasiveness, as "a little squib," but one that was "so not OK politically that I don't feel certain in advance that anyone will publish it."[2] Orwell was right to be doubtful: it was not until nearly a year after his essay on Koestler that *Animal Farm,* rejected in turn by Victor Gollancz, Jonathan Cape, and Faber and Faber, was finally published by the new firm of Secker and Warburg in August 1945.

In his essay "Why I Write," Orwell described the intention of *Animal Farm* in a succinct and often-quoted sentence. The book was "the first . . . in which I tried, with full consciousness of what I was doing, to fuse political purpose and artistic purpose into one whole."[3] His aesthetic purpose—to write, presumably, a book that would be praised as a work of art, attracting attention by its style and structure as much as by its content—was triumphantly vindicated by *Animal Farm*'s success. The four thousand copies issued by Secker and Warburg in 1945 sold out immediately, a second edition of ten thousand was printed,[4] and when *Animal Farm* was published in the United States a year later, it was selected by the Book-of-the-Month Club. It has established itself as a classic of modern fiction, and well within his lifetime it turned Orwell from a well-known writer into a famous one.

Clearly the eighteen-month gap—a large one in that period, even allowing for the wartime paper shortage—between the completion of *Animal Farm* and its publication did not result from any aesthetic inadequacy in the book. What caused the gap was the book's political purpose, which, as Orwell put it in his foreword to the Ukrainian edition of 1947, was nothing less than "the destruction of the Soviet myth," which Orwell felt to be "essential if we wanted a survival of the Socialist movement."[5] In Orwell's view, "the original idea of Socialism" had been corrupted by the false notion that Russia was "a Socialist country." He had realized the falsity of this notion in republican Spain, where communism operated not as a revolutionary force but as a mainstay of the middle-class status quo; he had also experienced its power to distort the perception of left-wingers outside the country of the Spanish war. It was on his return from Spain to Wallington in 1937, six years before he actually wrote his allegory of the decline of the Bolshevist revolution, that Orwell had first had a glimpse of the "animal fable" method he would eventually use: "One day . . . I saw a little boy, perhaps ten years old, driving a huge cart-horse along a narrow path, whipping it whenever it tried to turn. It struck me that if only such animals became aware of their strength, we should have no power over them, and that men exploit animals in much the same way as the rich exploit the proletariat."[6] The cart-horse turned into Orwell's indefatigable Boxer, but by 1943 and the thriving wartime alliance between Russia and the Western capitalist democracies Orwell must have nearly lost the small element of hope inherent in his "if only": for Boxer, and his fellow animals, are shown escaping the exploitation of the rich farmer Jones merely to fall victim to a hardly less cruel, and more depressing, exploitation by the pigs, who at the end of *Animal Farm* have become indistinguishable from him.

The alliance between Russia and the West seems to have created in Orwell a particularly urgent wish to publish his book without delay, as if to counteract the increasing media view of Stalin as a benevolent, whiskered "Uncle Joe," and the admiration provoked by the heroic struggle of the Red Army and the Russian people, from the recapture of Stalingrad in February 1943 to the relief of long-besieged Leningrad nearly a year later.[7] Unfortunately for Orwell, it was precisely the alliance with Russia that made publishers reluctant to accept his book. Though T. S. Eliot judged *Animal Farm* a good book, with a strong likeness to Swift's *Gulliver's Travels,* and recognized the "fundamental integrity" of Orwell's writing, he nevertheless felt on behalf of Faber and Faber that its political slant was inappropriate for the time.[8] The firm of Jonathan Cape had taken much the same line, even making at one point the "imbecile suggestion," in Orwell's view, "that some other animal than pigs might be made to represent the Bolsheviks."[9] By July 1944 Orwell was seriously considering publishing the book at his own expense, feeling that "it is important to get this book into print, and this year if possible."[10] In the same month, he expressed in *Tribune* his bitterness at the way in which, though no official censorship existed in Britain, unsuitable attitudes and information somehow failed to find an outlet: "the really well-trained dog is the one that turns his somersault when there is no whip."[11] But even the willingness of Secker and Warburg to print *Animal Farm* did not lead to publication until three months after the war in Europe had ended. Given Orwell's obvious wish to write a book that would not only recapitulate Russian history from 1917 to 1943, but that might have some influence, however slight, on current events, it is all the more remarkable that his aesthetic instinct was able to create a fictional world compelling enough to outlast its temporary application and transcend its particular material.

Why Orwell was able to do so is suggested by the responses of two of his friends. One, the poet and art historian Herbert Read, noted how accurately the allegorical narrative reflected the events of the Russian revolution without losing its naturalness as fiction: "The cap fits all round the head: everything is there, and yet there is no forcing of the story."[12] The other, the poet and critic William Empson, made a telling point that suggests not only the shades of political interpretation allowed by the book but also the range of emotional connotation involved in Orwell's choice of the animal fable as his modus operandi. Allegory, in Empson's view, was "a form that inherently means more than the author means, when it is handled sufficiently well."[13]

According to the varying predispositions of readers, argument may arise as to whether *Animal Farm* focuses essentially on the failure of the Russian revolution, or on the inherent likelihood of all revolutions to fail. Related to this may be uncertainty about whether the book points to particular historical causes for failure, the abuse of power by a particular class in particular circumstances, for instance; or to ineradicable flaws in human nature—the "darkness of man's heart" later explored by William Golding in *Lord of the Flies* (1954)—that may doom any society to less than perfection. Orwell's own intellectual view on the first matter, expressed in his essay on Arthur Koestler, was that "all revolutions are failures but they are not all the same failure";[14] and yet, though his story allegorizes Russia, the fact that its protagonists are "beasts of England" on an English farm is bound to pull against that external frame of reference. In the second matter, all one can say is that Orwell's agnostic humanism would probably have obliged him to reject the Christian pessimism of Golding, but that the residual Anglicanism that caused him to wish to be buried in a country churchyard would surely have enabled him to understand it. The idea, in Orwell's last book, of the future as "a boot stamping on a human face—for ever" seems at least as grounded in theological doctrines of innate depravity as in political second sight, and at the conclusion of *Animal Farm* one's sense of the human-faced, whip-carrying pigs as objects of the author's satire is outweighed by one's despairing pity for the animals looking on, and locked apparently forever into the brave new world to which the pigs' descent into "humanness" has brought them.

It is hard to understand how *Animal Farm* could ever have been described, as it was in the Penguin Books blurb a year after Orwell's death, as "a good-natured satire on dictatorship."[15] Whatever specifics Orwell meant to express, the haunting allegory in which he expressed them certainly "means more" as an autonomous creation, if only because in espousing the simplicity of language proper to a story about animals, he also unlocked a deeper level of emotional response than could have been reached by a detailed historical treatment of revolution. Paradoxically, the animal fable afforded Orwell a powerful vehicle in which to express his ideal of "human decency." Embodied in a human story, where complexities of character and motive must be treated, "decency" can seem as a political notion naive and sentimental; but for animals to attempt to attain a society based on it seems appropriate. When they fail, or are frustrated, in their attempt, what is evoked in the reader is more than regret: it is a naked sorrow at defenselessness. In chapter 9, when Boxer the cart-horse is carried off in the knacker's van, Orwell fuses allegory—the betrayed proletariat—so perfectly with story—a real horse treated with cruel ingratitude—that the nature of most readers' feelings must be as impossible to analyze as it is easy to imagine.

Reviewing *Animal Farm* in *Horizon,* Cyril Connolly expressed its mixture of elements by calling it "a fairy story told by a great lover of liberty and a great lover of animals."[16] Its moral and satiric thrust derive straightforwardly enough from the former aspect of Orwell. But much of the emotional power of the book is produced by its use for allegorical purposes of realistic animals, whose presentation Orwell could count on to tap a deep vein of protective sentiment in British readers. It is tempting to scholars and critics to adduce literary or folkloric sources for this responsiveness to animals in the works of Aesop and La Fontaine, but, though Orwell no doubt shared with some of his readers a knowledge of such writings, it seems probable that his, and their, feeling for animals had less "highbrow" origins: in nursery rhymes featuring animals, in the farm animal toys played with by children of Orwell's generation, and in such a children's book as Anna Sewell's *Black Beauty* (1877),[17] which combined a realistic and unsentimental picture of the lives of various types of horses with a high-minded Victorian inculcation of the need for kindness to animals. Given Orwell's admiration for such "Victorian" classics as *Uncle Tom's Cabin* and *Little Women,* it does not seem too farfetched to suppose that the simple clarity of *Black Beauty* may have provided him with a model of style, just as Swift's *Gulliver's Travels* and *A Tale of a Tub* are generally agreed to have influenced his allegorical approach.

Orwell was a "lover of animals" this side of idolatry, and his realistic presentation of them is as notable as their potential to involve the reader's emotions. It was from life more than from literature that Orwell drew his knowledge of animals, in common with those of his readers who had, or have, experienced farms either through a rural upbringing, through seeing animals in fields on trips into the country, or, in wartime Britain, as a result of evacuation in childhood from towns likely to be bombed to safe, though at first strange, agricultural areas. Like many children, Orwell had kept pets; in England he had shot rabbits (admitted as "comrades" in Animal Farm), in Burma pigeons, as well as the solitary elephant whose death he so movingly described in "Shooting an Elephant." Though he never ran a farm himself, the village where he lived from 1936 to 1940 was in farming country, and there he kept hens, a goat (whose name, Muriel, he used for the goat in *Animal Farm*), and a dog. His name for that dog, Marx, may have sparked Orwell's brilliantly simple notion of an entire farm—a society of animals controlled by humans—as an allegory first for capitalism, then for communism, which he calls "Animalism." It is surely no accident that the only place name that occurs in *Animal Farm,* the nearby small town of "Willingdon," closely resembles the name of Orwell's Hertfordshire village, Wallington.

That resemblance may explain the particular poignancy one recognizes in Orwell's occasional brief passages of landscape description in *Animal Farm,* that near the end of chapter 7 being the most lyrical. The revolution fails, but the place in which it fails reflected Orwell's memory of a country life that, for all its relative poverty, he had enjoyed and had associated with the last years of peace. But there is another, more sinister echo in Orwell's fictional location, which comes from further back and which, of all *Animal Farm*'s readers in 1945, perhaps only Cyril Connolly would have recognized: only three miles from Orwell's hated preparatory school, St. Cyprian's, lay the small Sussex village of Willingdon, on the other side of a downland hill of that name, which he could have looked toward from Eastbourne. Perhaps at least some of the unhappiness conveyed in *Animal Farm,* as well as some of its satire, flows out of memories of that oppressive system. Minimus's "Animal Farm" jingle in chapter 7, and the groveling poem to Napoleon in chapter 8, have the doggerel banality of English "school songs," and *Minimus* itself is the Latin term once used in school roll calls to distinguish the youngest of three attending siblings, the oldest, of course, being *Major,* like the prize old boar whose doctrines are so amended and reduced as the revolution goes on. Were "Sambo" and "Flip" the original autocratic pigs of Orwell's imaginative experience? He certainly had no love for real pigs, which is not the universal reaction. They are chosen to represent rulers in *Animal Farm* because of their intelligence, but also because of their greed and their cunning. When Orwell "tried the experiment of keeping a pig" on Jura in 1948, he found it "destructive and greedy," and displayed in his letters on the subject a dislike that verges on the vindictive: "They really are disgusting brutes and we are all longing for the day when he goes to the butcher."[18]

All of these various elements—external political reality, the complex of emotions evoked by animals, the throb of authorial memories—contribute a peculiar, often foreboding, intensity to Orwell's narrative, creating around it a penumbra of connotation. Orwell's subtitle, "A Fairy Story," may have been intended not only as an ironic comment on the book's historical relevance but also as an accurate indication of its poetic quality. But to say this is not to reduce the centrality of *Animal Farm*'s story line, which is admirably simple—crisp and grave by turns—in style, evenly paced, marked by rich inventiveness of phrase and incident, and skilled in offsetting the inevitability of its overall development by means of local suspense and surprises. Orwell's narrative clarity in *Animal Farm* may have owed something to his having obtained before publication the reaction of an attentive and intelligent reader: though he had never done so before with anyone else, Orwell discussed the book "in considerable detail" with his wife, Eileen, and told a friend she had helped in its planning.[19]

The use of the animal fable assisted Orwell not only with the atmosphere of his story, but with its scope and structure, enabling him both to boil down the complex details of political history to their essentials and to telescope them into memorable brevity. The Russian events, which took twenty-six years to unfold, from the anticapitalist revolution of 1917 to the rapprochement with capitalism in November 1943 (when Stalin met with Roosevelt and Churchill at the Teheran conference), are compressed in *Animal Farm* into ten short chapters covering nine or ten years, a credible equivalent in animal terms. The illicit night meeting with which the novel opens, at which the "wise and benevolent" old boar Major (Marx/Lenin) describes the exploitation of animals by humans and forecasts "a golden future time" of a world without humans, establishes the Soviet political allegory immediately by its statement that "all animals are comrades," while its other slogan, "all animals are equal," allows a wider reading, applicable alike to Jeffersonian idealism and British democratic socialism. Thus the abrupt abolition in chapter 7 of the stirring song "Beasts of England," an animal version of Blake's "Jerusalem," can be seen not only as a symbol of the decay of communist notions of a perfect state, but also, since at the end it is the once dreaded human beings the pig-rulers come to resemble, as Orwell's more general comment on the decline of true liberty and equality in the West.

The progress of the revolution from a common idealism to a two-tier, and later a three-tier, state system of leader, police, workers, takes only five chapters. Even before the drunken Mr. Jones is ousted by a spontaneous uprising sparked by hunger, and the feudally named "Manor Farm" becomes the egalitarian "Animal Farm" with its seven simple commandments and its green and white version of the Russian hammer and sickle flag, the pigs have emerged as natural organizers. When the hay harvest is gathered in (chap. 3), it is the other animals, particularly the two cart-horses, Boxer and Clover, who do the work, while the clever pigs, led by the strong, silent Napoleon (Stalin) and the intellectually innovative Snowball (Trotsky), not only supervise but keep for themselves all milk and apples on the grounds that they are good for the brain. For Orwell, the manipulative speech by which the propagandist porker, Squealer, justifies this to the other animals was the key passage of *Animal Farm*:[20] it demonstrates both the greed and the hypocrisy involved in the urge to power, which disguises itself as sacrifice for the common good. At first, the reader shares in the euphoria and pride of the animals in their early period of success and freedom from obvious oppression. When this reaches its climax in the triumphant, mock-heroic "Battle of the Cowshed" (chap. 4), the reader can admire alike the strength of Boxer and the courage and strategic skill of Snowball, both of whom are awarded the newly created order "Animal Hero, First Class."[21] But there are ominous undercurrents even here. The decent Boxer, thinking he has killed a stable lad, is sorry; for Snowball the death does not matter. In this divergence is visible the gap that gradually widens between the pigs—who first put forward all the resolutions at the democratic Sunday meetings (chap. 3) and then take over all policy decisions on the farm (chap. 4)—and the rank-and-file animal workers, who accept direction with naive optimism.

The distinction between rulers and ruled is given more brutal form in chapter 5, at the end of only the first year of the revolution, when the constant disagreement between Napoleon and Snowball on matters of policy comes to a head. In foreign policy, represented by Animal Farm's relationship with its human-run neighbors, Foxwood and Pinchfield, Napoleon favors a defensive buildup of armaments, Snowball an attempt at destabilization by propaganda. Domestically, Napoleon urges increased food production, Snowball the building of a windmill that, when finished, will reduce working hours. When Snowball's eloquence threatens to win the day, Napoleon suddenly calls up a pack of fierce dogs who chase Snowball off the farm—a simplified reenactment of Trotsky's expulsion from Russia in 1929. Henceforth the leader principle replaces democracy: reared up from puppies in secret, the dogs are as exclusively loyal to Napoleon as their predecessors had been to Mr. Jones. "Meetings" are immediately abolished, being replaced by weekly "Orders" drawn up by Napoleon and a select politburo of pigs. Animal Farm is now run by a mixture of intimidation and chicanery, the dogs of the KGB ever ready to growl down dissent, Squealer always on hand to extol Napoleon, any failure in whose selfless vigilance, the other animals are persuaded, will result in the return of the hated Jones.

Chapters 6 through 9, covering three more years, chart a progressive and irreversible decline, which is shown in three main ways, all interrelated and amounting to a bitter gloss on the phrase that opens chapter 6: "All that year the animals worked like slaves." The "like" is seen as more and more superfluous: the animals *are* slaves, to their own noble idealism, to the regime that dupes and mistreats them, and to the loss of memory the regime's rewriting of history brings about. Napoleon first appropriates Snowball's plans for a windmill, which in Soviet terms represent industrialization, then claims Snowball stole them from him; similarly, Snowball's role in the Battle of the Cowshed is bit by bit downgraded until at last he is represented as having led the opposing, human forces. Like Trotsky, Snowball is turned into the arch-criminal and convenient bogy, and in chapter 7, a grimly vivid miniature of the Soviet purges of the 1930s, a number of animals, including four porkers, and some hens who have opposed Napoleon's collectivization, are seized and executed after confessing they have been in league with Snowball. The event leaves the other animals "shaken and miserable," but as much over the "treachery" they credit as over the "cruel retribution" they have witnessed. Yet loyalty, obedience and discipline, the watchwords of Animal Farm since chapter 5, do not guarantee gratitude. When Boxer, whose personal slogans are "I will work harder" and "Napoleon is always right," collapses under a load of stone for the windmill, he is cheated of the promised retirement he has earned. Instead, he is carted off to the knacker's (chap.9), to a death that, in effect, turns him into food for dogs and "another case of whisky for the pigs." Though at the time the other animals utter "a cry of horror" and try to warn him, they are all too easily convinced by Squealer later that "our leader, Comrade Napoleon" could not possibly have let such a thing happen.

The blurring of the past and the hardening shape of the present, grim, greedy, or just pragmatic, are accompanied by a betrayal of the spirit of the revolution exemplified in the amendments made to its letter, the "seven commandments" of "Animalism" promulgated in chapter 2. Constantly these are changed, just before the puzzled animals can check their uneasy memories against them, to keep pace with the increasing decadence and authoritarianism of the pigs. Hence in turn, "No animal shall sleep in a bed" becomes, when the pigs move into the farmhouse in chapter 6, "No animal shall sleep in a bed with sheets," and after the savage killings in chapter 7, "No animal shall kill any other animal" is modified by the addition of "without cause."

This insidious process of formal tinkering reaches its brilliant, and depressing, climax at the end of the book. More and more the pigs have gravitated toward the human world, first through trade and alliances (the selling of timber to Mr. Frederick of Pinchfield is the animal equivalent of the short-lived Nazi-Soviet nonaggression pact of 1939); then, as they celebrate their Pyrrhic victory over him at "the Battle of the Windmill" (chap. 8), through drinking alcohol. More and more has Napoleon, "elected" president in chapter 9, become the remote object of a personality cult in a system marked by "re-adjustment" of rations for workers and the empty "dignity" of "more songs, more speeches, more processions." The two trends meet and fuse in chapter 10, set a few years later on in a world where almost none remember either "the old days before the Rebellion" or the period of freedom immediately after it. Prosperity has come, but only to the pigs and the dogs; for the rest "life was as it had always been." Despite this, the animals still retain hope for the earthly millenium when "the green fields of England should be untrodden by human feet," still hum the proscribed "Beasts of England" in secret, and still take pride in the fact that "they were not as other animals. If they were hungry, it was not from feeding tyrannical human beings; if they worked hard, at least they worked for themselves. No creature among them went upon two legs. No creature called any other creature 'Master'. All animals were equal" (62).

The paragraph from which this passage comes is among the most eloquent pieces of writing in all Orwell's work. It is a statement that, though it sits well with the particular Soviet allegory of *Animal Farm,* also rises strongly out of it to present a universal notion of liberty. For Orwell, it is the proletariat, rather than the politicians or the intelligentsia, who keep the flame of idealism alive. Yet, in the context Orwell has built up, the belief is no more than a pathetic dream, and its last phrase is like a tree waiting for the axe. The axe falls almost immediately. Squealer, then the other pigs, then Napoleon, emerge from the farmhouse walking on two legs; the latter carries a whip, the hated symbol of human beings, in his trotter. The mob of sheep, whose chant used to be "Four legs good, two legs bad," have been coached to chant "Four legs good, two legs *better,*" the identical verbal pattern expressing a completely opposite meaning. Yet this *has* a meaning, however horrifying in the context. The ultimate verbal expression of tyranny is linguistic nonsense, and on the wall of the barn the one remaining commandment is Orwell's magnificent and unforgettable example of it: "All animals are equal, but some animals are more equal than others." The reader's amusement at the cleverness of this Wildean trope is quickly smothered under the weight of the facts and events it implies. The final animal-human banquet, Orwell's version of the Teheran conference, drives home the stark contrast between hope and reality, as Mr. Pilkington, the capitalist West, praises the "discipline and orderliness" of Animal Farm, and utters the bon mot that widens the book to more than an anti-Communist allegory: "If you have your lower animals to contend with . . . we have our lower classes." With the announced change of name back to "Manor Farm," the revolution has come full circle, and however the two groups, pigs and humans, may quarrel, they look the same to the animals gazing in, the working classes who, it seems, are betrayed by all governments.

One draws that last inference uneasily. Had Orwell gone ahead in 1944 and brought out *Animal Farm* at his own expense, he intended to preface it with an essay containing this sentence: "If liberty means anything at all it means the right to tell people what they do not wish to hear."[22] His anxiety to show the Soviet system in its true colors—how after its pretensions to a greater liberty, it merely approximated capitalism and reintroduced hierarchy in a new guise—causes his allegorical method to imply stronger criticism of the Western allies, and of Roosevelt and Churchill, than one can believe he fully intended. Nevertheless, the eagerness of Mr. Pilkington and his neighbors to "introduce on their own farms" the harsher regime of the pigs (65) strikes a sinister note, and reflects the fear shown in many of Orwell's essays that liberty would diminish everywhere if vigilance relaxed.[23]

Good allegories, as William Empson told Orwell in 1945, are apt to mean "more than their authors mean"; allegories may also mean things the author does not mean. Allegory distorts as well as simplifies, as critics, including Orwell himself, have felt about book 4 of *Gulliver's Travels.* On the whole, the allegory of *Animal Farm* works well enough in terms of Orwell's topical intention, to discredit the Soviet system by showing its inhumanity and its back-sliding from ideals Orwell valued and still hoped could be achieved. The Swiftian element in the book lies only partly in the doubts it casts on that hope; it lies also in its rich fictional inventiveness, the scores of small details—the burial of the hams in chapter 2, the "reverent" filing past Major's skull in chapter 5, the ribbons of Mollie and the ribbons of the pigs—by which allegorical purpose is given a local habitation in a sharply visualized community of animals.

It is this sharpness of visualization and the emotional resonance it creates that have ensured *Animal Farm* what seems likely to be a permanent place in literature. Mixing, as Bernard Crick has well expressed it, "serenity of tone" and "bitterness of content,"[24] it is neither simple allegory nor simple animal fable. Graham Greene rightly noted in his review that we "become involved in the fate" of the animals.[25] We care about them too much merely to translate events into their historical equivalent. Reading the fables of Aesop and La Fontaine, we are sufficiently distant to be able to laugh at the dupe as well as to reprimand the trickster. There is no such possibility in *Animal Farm,* nor, by the end, can we escape the weight of the book's sadness by thinking that these things have only happened to animals. We look from the oppressed animals in the book to the oppressed human beings outside and back again, and can see no difference.

Chapter Seven

The Last Man in Europe: *Nineteen Eighty-Four*

When, at the end of 1948, Fredric Warburg received from Orwell the manuscript of his last novel, he summed up his response in the very first sentence of his publisher's report: "This is amongst the most terrifying books I have ever read."[1] This view, by and large, has found an echo in many critics in the last four decades, and it seems likely that the book's bleak presentation of a totalitarianism unredeemed by any public-spirited motive whatever was the main factor in its rapid assumption of classic status. In its first year of publication it sold over four hundred thousand copies; by the actual year 1984 it had sold over eleven million.[2]

In that year, when the appearance of so many pieces on Orwell unintentionally emphasized the historical 1984's difference from his fictional version, Bernard Crick brought out an edition of the novel with a massive apparatus of introduction and annotation. Much of this is very valuable, especially in consolidating a more recent sense of the novel as a reflection of the straitened war years during which it gestated, and the uncertain, fearful postwar world in which it was written. Whether or not one still considers *Nineteen Eighty-Four* a prophecy of future time—the general view when it appeared—it can now be seen as very much a product of its own. While usefully modifying the "received" view of the novel, however, Crick expresses a wish that "those teaching the text could try to recover a sense of how *funny* much of it is.[3] "Recover" is misleading: the record of previous criticism hardly reveals that such a view of the book was ever taken, let alone lost. Despite elements of the melodramatic villain in some of O'Brien's speeches to Winston Smith in part 3, I can find no evidence to support such a radically new reading. Even if "terrifying" now seems too strong, "funny" is decidedly not the word to apply to *Nineteen Eighty-Four.*

Orwell drafted his earliest notes for what became *Nineteen Eighty-Four* some time in 1943, under the heading "The Last Man in Europe."[4] He had in mind at that time a book in two parts; firmly established already were the notion of the "Two Minutes' Hate," the protagonist's relationship with two other characters, and a future society based on "organized lying," in which "objective truth" had disappeared. These last phenomena had first become apparent to Orwell during his time in Spain when, in his view, the P.O.U.M. was systematically misrepresented, and many of his essays of the 1940s are haunted by the recurrent fear that history was vulnerable to alteration for political ends.

By the spring of 1944 Orwell was revealing further aspects of his fear of the shape the future seemed to be assuming. A review of two books that respectively defended laissez-faire capitalism and attacked it—F. A. Hayek's *The Road to Serfdom* and K. Zilliacus's *The Mirror of the Past*—showed Orwell aware of the horrors attendant on either of the two systems advocated: "Capitalism leads to dole queues, the scramble for markets, and war. Collectivism leads to concentration camps, leader worship, and war."[5] For Orwell, the only "way out" was a depressingly unlikely compromise whereby "a planned economy can be somehow combined with the freedom of the intellect, which can only happen if the concept of right and wrong is restored to politics." There is no sign of this in the repressive society of *Nineteen Eighty-Four,* which fulfills the grim prophecy offered by Hayek: "By bringing the whole of life under the control of the state, Socialism necessarily gives power to an inner ring of bureaucrats [Orwell's "Inner Party"], who in almost every case will be men who want power for its own sake and will stick at nothing in order to retain it." Later the same month (April 1944), in his *Tribune* "As I Please" column, Orwell warned of the fallacy of supposing that, "under a dictatorial government," the individual could remain "free *inside,*" as Bozo the pavement artist once could. His image—drawn from European fascism—of a "totalitarianism . . . visibly on the up-grade in every part of the world" was to be reproduced almost exactly in the novel he made his first start on a year later: "Out in the street the loudspeakers bellow, the flags flutter from the rooftops, the police with their tommy-guns prowl to and fro, the face of the Leader, four feet wide, glares from every hoarding."[6]

Orwell's notion of the increasing ubiquity of totalitarianism derived not only from his awareness of the actual regimes in Italy, Germany, and Russia, but also from his reading of a book very influential in the 1940s, James Burnham's *The Managerial Revolution.* This postulated a future in which technocratic "managers" would take over from politicians, and where "politics consists of the struggle for power, and nothing else." The world in which this "struggle" would take place, the logical result of expansionist tendencies already operative, would consist not of "a patchwork of small, independent states, but of great super-states grouped around the main industrial centres in Europe, Asia and America."[7] Orwell reviewed Burnham's book in an essay, "Second Thoughts on James Burnham," published in *Polemic* in May 1946; but as Orwell's title indicates, Burnham's ideas had entered his mind earlier than that. A letter two years before had described "the sort of world that I am afraid of," in terms precisely premonitory of *Nineteen Eighty-Four*: "a world of two or three great superstates which are unable to conquer one another," in which "two and two could become five if the fuehrer wished it."[8] Orwell stated a similar view in October 1945 in a *Tribune* essay entitled "You and the Atom Bomb,"[9] but his grimmest version of it was expressed in an essay published in the American *Partisan Review* in the summer of 1947. Entitled "Toward European Unity," it put forward three unpleasant possibilities for the postwar world, only avoidable by an attempt to make true "democratic Socialism work throughout some large area." But the "actual outlook" seemed to Orwell to be "very dark," and his third and "worst possibility" deserves to be quoted in full. It was:

> That the fear inspired by the atomic bomb and other weapons yet to come will be so great that everyone will refrain from using them. . . . It would mean the division of the world among two or three vast super-states, unable to conquer one another and unable to be overthrown by any internal rebellion. In all probability their structure would be hierarchic, with a semi-divine caste at the top and outright slavery at the bottom, and the crushing out of liberty would exceed anything the world has yet seen. Within each state the necessary psychological atmosphere would be kept up by a complete severance from the outside world, and by a continuous phony war against rival states. Civilizations of this type might remain static for thousands of years.[10]

The Burnhamesque prediction made here is almost identical with the world presented by *Nineteen Eighty-Four,* work on which Orwell resumed in May 1947, having made a serious start on it the previous summer. A fictional reinforcement of Orwell's worldview had by that time also been contributed by his reading a French translation of the novel *We* (in English, *My*) by the Russian novelist E. I. Zamyatin (1884–1937). This novel, set in the twenty-sixth century, in an urban, totalitarian society hostile to the imagination, was reviewed by Orwell at the beginning of 1946 in *Tribune.* Orwell saw it as "superior" to Aldous Huxley's far better known *Brave New World* (1932) because it had an "intuitive grasp of the irrational side of totalitarianism—human sacrifice, cruelty as an end in itself, the worship of a Leader [called in *We* "the Benefactor"] who is credited with divine attributes."[11] In recognizing such elements, Orwell's novel is far closer to *We* than to the bland, scientific un-freedom of *Brave New World*; Orwell's novel also shares with *We* a love relationship, truncated by the state, between two rebels. But in important ways *Nineteen Eighty-Four* is unlike its Russian "analogue." Whereas *We* depicts a system that is struggled against by many revolutionaries, *Nineteen Eighty-Four* offers only the futile rebellion of two individuals against a backdrop of Party conformity and proletarian powerlessness. The Slavic scholar E. J. Brown, summing up the difference in tone between the two books, acutely locates the depression evident in *Nineteen Eighty-Four.* Whereas "Zamyatin's mood is one of ironic contempt for collectivists and cosmists," Orwell "was afraid of his enemy, exaggerated his power, and tried to communicate to the reader his own apprehension."[12]

Taken in terms of their discursive presentation in various of his letters, essays, and reviews, Orwell's theoretical concerns about the likely shape of the future can be considered as the stuff of which political satire is made. Orwell did, in fact, once describe *Nineteen Eighty-Four* as "a satire"; but that was in a letter he sent to an American trade union official in order to counter a view of the book that had greatly distressed him, that it was "an attack on Socialism or on the British Labour Party."[13] In this context, *satire* may have been intended as a less worrying term, perhaps because it would sound more "literary." It seems also, though, to have been meant to reinforce a sense of the book as open-ended: the book did not prophesy that "the kind of society I describe necessarily *will* arrive," but warned that "something resembling it *could* arrive," even in Britain, "if not fought against." Orwell underlined that last phrase, thus suggesting the positive aim synonymous with satire. Yet it is hard for the recipient of Orwell's vision to distinguish between its author's purpose and his book's effect. In choosing to set his novel in a dated future, especially one not far off, Orwell may have intended the message "Strive to avoid *this*"; but what the reader experiences is a society that *has* arrived, and that offers within itself no hints as to how it may be avoided. One may choose—because desperate to believe its picture farfetched—to call *Nineteen Eighty-Four* a satire; but none of it invites laughter (as many satires do), or an efficacious disapproval, and it certainly cannot be called, as E. J. Brown calls *We,* "a confident and triumphant satire."[14] The sociopolitical elements from Burnham and Zamyatin that fed into Orwell's book are only part of the story; or rather, perhaps, they are the story but not its tone. Though it would be hazardous and simplistic to draw too definite a connecting link, it is difficult to escape the sense that *Nineteen Eighty-Four*'s tone—a powerful, gloomy undercurrent of loss, nostalgia, and even guilt—derives not from Orwell's political thinking, his rational fears of the future, but from the emotions generated by his personal situation in the 1940s.

That much of *Nineteen Eighty-Four*'s general physical setting—a gray, gritty, depressing London of shortages, inconvenience, ruined building, and occasional rocket bombs—derives from the actual London of the war years has been amply demonstrated by a number of Orwell's recent commentators, notably Bernard Crick in his edition of the novel and W. J. West in his edition of Orwell's BBC broadcasts.[15] Many specifics relate to Orwell's BBC years from 1941 to 1943. The canteen at Winston Smith's place of work, the Ministry of Truth, is drawn from the BBC canteen (which had a dish called "Victory Pie") in the converted department store near Oxford Circus where Orwell worked. The enormous Ministry of Truth itself, three hundred meters high, is an exaggeration of the wartime Ministry of Information, housed in what was at that time the tallest building in London, the Senate House of London University: like Winston Smith from Victory Mansions, Orwell could see this from the window of one of the successive apartments he lived in during the war. As an employee of the BBC, Orwell had some experience of the censorship exerted at one remove by the ministry on broadcasting policy; it has been plausibly suggested that his fictional term "Big Brother"derived from the name of the Minister of Information, Brendan Bracken, known to his subordinates as "B. B."[16] Orwell's fictional abbreviations—Miniluv, Minipax, Minitrue, Miniplenty—copy the real telegraphic address used by the Ministry of Information, "Miniform."

To have recorded such elements of wartime restraint and curtailment as continuing to exist, in intenser forms, some forty years in the future would indicate, despite the resilience still evident in his nonfictional prose, the extent to which Orwell's imagination had come to feel menaced by the postwar present in which he wrote *Nineteen Eighty-Four.* Much of the book's blackness has, not unnaturally, been attributed to Orwell's poor state of health at the time, especially as he outlived its publication by only seven months. Between the time he finished the rough draft (October 1947) and when he resumed work to bring it to final form stretched another seven-month period, spent in a hospital near Glasgow with tuberculosis of the lung. Two months before Orwell sent the completed text (typed out by himself with difficulty) to Frederic Warburg, he described the book as "a good idea but the execution would have been better if I had not written it under the influence of T. B."[17] It is hard to know whether Orwell meant by "influence" something strictly physical, and by "execution" matters of technique only, or whether he was conceding that his health had affected the book's whole conception and atmosphere. Reading part 3, for instance, one may feel that Winston's long period of timelessness and torture in the Ministry of Love (with beside him "a man in a white coat, holding a hypodermic syringe" [881]) has distinct undertones of hospital experience, and that, though Winston's emaciation results in the novel from brutality and deprivation, it approximates convincingly the state of a man terminally ill ("at a guess he would have said that it was the body of a man of sixty, suffering from some malignant disease" [900]). But whatever the degree of "influence" brought to bear on *Nineteen Eighty-Four* by Orwell's health, other factors existed that, even without the physical one, could hardly have failed to affect his emotional state when contemplating the future. Winston Smith, in 1984, not only tries to reconstruct the past so continuously revised by the Party, and by himself in the Ministry of Truth, but—most unusually for Orwell—is shown dreaming about it, as early as part 1, chapter 3. Perhaps the deepest and most nagging fear conveyed by *Nineteen Eighty-Four* is the fear of the disappearance of the past. Winston Smith's recurrent, haunting dreams of his dead, or disappeared, family show him to be irrevocably cut off from it; as was Orwell by the time he began writing his novel.

The years from 1939 to 1946 were punctuated, for Orwell, by a sequence of family deaths that, even for an undemonstrative son and brother, can hardly have failed to reinforce the war's own closing of doors on the past. Orwell's father had died of cancer in June 1939 at the age of eighty-two; Orwell's mother followed him in March 1943 at only sixty-eight: Orwell was present at both deaths. Much is made, in *Nineteen Eighty-Four,* of Winston Smith's loss of his mother, who in part 2, chapter 7 is described as having had "an air of nobility" and as one to whom "it would not have occurred . . . that an action which is ineffectual thereby becomes meaningless" (841)—descriptions that, intended to suggest past values, apply accurately to the self-regulated virtues of the Victorian age. To Winston's haunting memories of his mother is added guilt about his sick younger sister, whose chocolate ration he stole, returning later to find her and his mother vanished. How far such a fictional incident reflects personal experience it is impossible to say, although—like the uneasy feelings Gordon Comstock has toward his sister in *Keep the Aspidistra Flying*—it may originate in some sense of unfair male privilege, specifically over the proportion of the Blair family finances devoted to Eric Blair's education. What is clear, however, is that Orwell's serious work on *Nineteen Eighty-Four* began not long after the death of his elder sister, Marjorie, his playmate of Henley days, at the early age of forty-eight. It was only a few days after attending her funeral, in May 1946, that Orwell traveled north to the place where the novel was written, the remote Scottish island of Jura in the Inner Hebrides.

On his way there he stopped to visit his wife's grave. Eileen Blair had not lived to see in print the book on which she had been so helpful, *Animal Farm.* Instead, on 29 March 1945, she had died while under anaesthetic for an operation—in fact a complete hysterectomy—to remove a growth on the uterus.[18] Eileen had feared for some time that she had cancer, but had not told her husband; with the result that her death, in Newcastle-upon-Tyne, caught him unprepared, and absent in Europe reporting the end of the war for the *Observer.* He had himself been taken ill while in Cologne, and discharged himself from hospital on hearing his wife was dead; though, conscientious and in need of distraction, he returned later to Germany, then Paris, to complete his assignment. From Paris, in May 1945, he wrote to a friend that "the destruction in Germany is terrifying, far worse than people in England grasp."[19] Though, characteristically, Orwell neither expressed grief to his friends nor slackened in his work as a journalist, it does not seem farfetched to infer, from the atmosphere and details of *Nineteen Eighty-Four,* that he took with him to Jura in May 1945 a powerful sense of personal loss and many eyewitness images of a world reduced to grayness and rubble.

Orwell's move to a Scottish island had been long contemplated. A wartime diary entry (20 June 1940) speaks longingly of "my islands in the Hebrides, which I suppose I shall never possess or even see . . . even now most of the islands are uninhabited . . . and most have water and a little cultivable land, and goats will live on them."[20] It was through David Astor, son of the *Observer*'s proprietor who owned land there, that Orwell and his wife, in 1944, became aware of the island of Jura: an abandoned farmhouse called Barnhill was available for renting at the northern end of the island, the one closest to the mainland as the crow flies yet as far as possible from the ferry terminal. Barnhill itself was situated at the end of a rutted five-mile track almost impassable for vehicles.

Because of Barnhill's remoteness, the gloomy nature of what Orwell wrote there, and an incorrect notion of Jura's climate as damp and bitter, Orwell's decision to live in such a place, given his poor health, was for a long time treated by commentators as a death wish. Bernard Crick has crisply scouted this view in his biography, stating that "elaborate critical theories of Orwell's character and of his last writings have been built on isothermic fantasy": in fact "the climate was mild."[21] On his arrival there, Orwell pronounced Barnhill "a lovely house,"[22] As well as satisfying Orwell's wish to bring up his and Eileen's adopted son Richard away from the metropolis, Jura was a place where he could escape the pressures of his journalism and "get on with another book."[23] It must also have represented, in a world growing ever more threatening and regimented, an escape to simplicity and naturalness—in effect, a return to a past style of life, perhaps even to Orwell's Scots identity as Blair. Yet Jura's remoteness, in one way a healing influence, may well have had an important drawback. In choosing, over the summers and autumns of 1946, 1947, and 1948, to concentrate on writing down his vision of the future in a place so very distant from the political centers in which that future was being shaped, Orwell may have plunged, for want of the day-to-day modifications furnished by a diverse experience of people, ever deeper into the somber recesses of his own theoretical fears. The price, in imaginative terms, that Orwell paid for his understandable wish to get away from postwar London was a high one.

In his publisher's report on *Nineteen Eighty-Four,* Frederic Warburg found "one weak link in Orwell's construction." This was that Orwell "nowhere indicated how man, English man, becomes bereft of his humanity."[24] Since the novel leaves no doubt of the methods by which Winston Smith (and any other dissidents) are either eliminated or reduced to automata by the "Thought Police," what Warburg presumably found hard to accept was how the "Inner Party" (whose instrument the Thought Police are) had reached the position of subsisting on the exercise of power purely for its own sake, with all other normal human motivations excluded. This reservation about the book has been ex-

pressed more recently by Bernard Crick, together with another: "Could a totalitarian regime destroy objective truth?"[25] A related objection was lodged by Harold Nicolson, reviewing *Nineteen Eighty-Four* just after its publication in June 1949: he was unable to credit either that people would have forgotten the pre-"Ingsoc" (pre-1960) past so quickly, or that the Thought Police could so completely monitor the lives of the "Outer Party" members who make up 13 percent of the population. For these reasons he found the book "not convincing."[26]

Nevertheless, Nicolson pronounced it "impressive," essentially because the circumstantial texture of the novel powerfully conveyed "the awful twilight of the mind" in a repressive regime. Set against this, his objections have a theoretical ring to them, and even against the profounder points raised by Warburg and Crick must be set the former's "terrifying" and the latter's view that *Nineteen Eighty-Four* is at the very least a warning that cannot by brushed aside. These three commentators have been by no means alone in withholding total intellectual assent from the assumptions seen to underlie Orwell's view of the future; but their *post factum* disagreements, and those of others, plainly sit side by side with an emotional involvement, which continues after the book is finished, that cannot be rationalized away. It seems a fair guess that such a response to *Nineteen Eighty-Four*'s power as fiction continues to operate. Though the world has passed the year 1984 without turning into a comprehensive factual simulacrum of Orwell's predictions of possibility, torture flourishes, methods of surveillance have multiplied, and the "blue overalls which were the uniform of the Party" (743) have long had their equivalents in China. What Philip Rahv said of the novel in 1949 is no less true today: "If it inspires dread above all, that is precisely because its materials are taken from the real world as we know it."[27]

Selected and intensified, these materials combine to powerful effect in *Nineteen Eighty-Four.* Orwell's fears about the future may have been theoretical—and thus are open to argument—but his embodiment of them in character and environment gives them an authority hard to escape, except by sharing in the stratagems of the main character, Winston Smith—stratagems that the developing narrative not only renders futile but reveals to have been doomed from the start. From the very first sentence—"It was a bright cold day in April, and the clocks were striking thirteen"—the reader is plunged into a world both recognizable and strange, but not so strange as to be implausible or to sound like science fiction. It can be cold in an English April, and the twenty-four-hour clock had been introduced for some official purposes during World War II; nevertheless the juxtaposition suggests an alteration not only of social, but of natural, laws—a sinister change, since thirteen is an unlucky number. Nature, it becomes clear from part 2, has not in fact changed, and in the brief excursion of Winston and his lover Julia into the country it provides a moment of radiant affirmation (816–17) akin to that of Orwell's essay "Some Thoughts on the Common Toad" (1946); but this excursion is unique. Apart from it, and from one later, ecstatic response to "the pale, cloudless sky, stretching away beyond the chimney-pots into interminable distance" (868), the subversive freedom of nature is simply not offered as an available alternative in the novel. Instead, there is urban decrepitude and joyless Party conformity; or there is the heavily guarded, windowless Ministry of Love. The three parts of *Nineteen Eighty-Four* depict Winston Smith's inevitable journey from the one to the other, and its defeated conclusion in the ironically named "Chestnut Tree Café."[28] If he had chosen to give the three parts titles, they could well have borne the titles used by Orwell's near-contemporary Elizabeth Bowen for her tripartite novel of 1938, *The Death of the Heart*: "The World," "The Flesh," "The Devil." The first two, approximately the same length, focus in turn on the claustrophobic world of which Winston is an unwilling part, and on the intensely physical love relationship with Julia, a fellow "Outer Party" member, that provides a temporary escape from it. In the shorter last section, Winston encounters in and through the "Inner Party" member O'Brien the naked urge to power that lies at the heart of "Ingsoc," the unrecognizably debased "English Socialism" that governs Oceania and "Airstrip One"—as England, with a spurt of anti-Americanism on Orwell's part, is called in the novel.

The reader's immersion in the dark world of Airstrip One, with its poor food, dingy buildings, two-way "telescreens," and the ubiquitous watching face of Big Brother, is made more claustrophobic because of the novel's adoption virtually throughout of a single viewpoint: Winston Smith is not merely its protagonist but its sole mind and mediator. The only variation from his angle of vision is some twenty pages that Orwell's American publishers, fearing they would deter the Book-of-the-Month Club from choosing the novel, wished him to cut out: the excerpts, introduced into part 2, from the essay "The Theory and Practice of Oligarchical Collectivism," purportedly by Emmanuel Goldstein, the Trotsky figure[29] who is daily vilified during the "Two Minutes' Hate";[30] and Orwell's authorial description, printed as an appendix, of "The Principles of Newspeak," the Party's official language. The first text, based on the forecasts of James Burnham, provides the origin and rationale of the world of *Nineteen Eighty-Four*; the second not only comments on verbal formulae occurring in the novel, as for instance during Winston Smith's "rectification" work at the Ministry of Truth, but explains what lies behind them: the Party's intention to suppress all dissent ("Thoughtcrime") by eliminating words, and word senses, that could express it. In refusing to cut these passages, Orwell indicated his own view of their importance in the novel: their omission "would alter the whole colour of the book and leave out much that is essential."[31] They are, indeed, of considerable intrinsic interest: Orwell's essay on "Newspeak," particularly, has continued to exert a fascination as sheer linguistic invention that threatens to undercut its deeper warning about mind-control. Orwell's claim, made in 1949, that the two passages were "essential" suggests a wish, after the event, to present *Nineteen Eighty-Four* as a treatise, perhaps because, having written the book, he had exorcised the obsessions and personal losses that had contributed to its making. What the two sections provide for the reader, however, is less a necessary theoretical underpinning to the story than, through the coolness of their tone, a species of safety valve from it. Yet is is too much to claim that their absence would change "the whole colour" of the book, since the few pages of their presence only lighten its black momentarily to gray.

The degree to which Winston Smith's world is circumscribed is indicated by one of O'Brien's statements to him in part 3: "It is intolerable to us that an erroneous thought should exist anywhere in the world, however secret and powerless it may be" (890). By itself such a statement sounds more than arrogant and intolerant: it verges on the clinically insane. But *Nineteen Eighty-Four* offers no evidence of successful dissent to set against it: even apparently loyal supporters of the regime, such as Winston's fellow workers Syme, Ampleforth, and Parsons (the latter in his sleep), stray into error, are arrested, and presumably are "vaporized." Compared with their "rebellion," Winston Smith's is huge and glaring because intentional; the reader shares it not only because he cannot get outside Winston's perspective but because he is invited to participate, both by the name "Smith," which conveys "Everyman" normality, and by the name "Winston," with its Churchillian overtones of heroic individuality. The latter name, particularly for the reader of 1949, presents Orwell's protagonist, born about 1945, as a last survivor, projected into a future from which he strains through mist to remember what the reader is still part of. The very diary in which Winston attempts to record his thoughts and experiences, thus asserting what Newspeak dismissively labels "Ownlife," is a fragment of the past (746), and whereas at work he enters fully into the Party's constant "re-inscription" of the "palimpsest" of history (part 1, chapter 4), at home and in his illicit forays into "prole" districts and Mr. Charrington's junk shop (part 1, chapter 8), he tries to discover, through talk and objects, evidence to support his "ancestral memory that things had once been different" (778). To some degree, in fact, this subversive independence surfaces in Winston's work too, as in his invention of the zealous "Comrade Ogilvy" who "had no subjects of conversation except the principles of Ingsoc" (770): the description verges on parody, and offers, like his diary entries, a glimpse of Winston as a frustrated creative writer in a society where literature has degenerated into Party dogma on the one hand and machine-written "Prolefeed" on the other.

The proles themselves—who form 85 percent of the population, live in poverty and ignorance, and are considered harmless by the Thought Police—have retained many of the decent values, particularly those concerned with personal and family relationships, that the Party has done its best to eliminate in its members. Toward the end of part 1, Winston confides to his diary the thought: "If there is any hope . . . it lies in the proles" (783), and on two occasions in part 2 the sight of a large, fertile prole woman, singing as she pegs out diapers, reinforces his feeling that the proles constitute a natural force capable of overwhelming the Party. The proles of *Nineteen Eighty-Four* bear some resemblance to the working classes as presented in "The Art of Donald McGill," and critics looking for a way out of the depressing closed world of Ingsoc have sometimes ascribed Winston's view to Orwell himself. The novel, however, never offers a glimmer of their potential issuing in action, and at one point (part 1, chapter 8) Winston describes his "hope" about the proles as both "the statement of a mystical truth and a palpable absurdity" (791)—a classic example of "Doublethink," the mental habit prized by the Party, one form of which involves the simultaneous holding of two contradictory opinions.

Neither the proles nor his search for the past provides Winston with a real escape from his regulated life as a Party member, only an escape in the mind, since "Nothing was your own except the few cubic centimeters inside your skull" (758). Before he discovers in part 3 that this mental freedom, too, is denied him, his relationship with Julia, which dominates Part 2, offers him a physical happiness he knows cannot last—since adultery between Party members is forbidden—but which, while it prospers, is the nearest the novel approaches to normality. On the surface, Julia is an orthodox Party member, a zealous activist of the Junior Anti-Sex League; beneath it, she harbors a violent hatred of the Party, of which her affair with Winston—which she initiates by smuggling him a note—is not the first expression. Her hostility, however, is a matter of instinct rather than intellect: in Winston's phrase, she is "only a rebel from the waist downwards" (836), fully aware of the Party's use of sexual repression to foment hysterical loyalty, but remaining sane because of her "lack of understanding" of, and lack of interest in, the broader ramifications of Party doctrine and "the difference between truth and falsehood" (834). At first "a physical necessity" to Winston, she soon inspires in him "a deep tenderness" (826) that conceivably (since this is the only comprehensively described love relationship in Orwell's work) embodies Orwell's memories of his dead wife Eileen.[32] Their one excursion outside London (part 2, chapter 2) brings to life for Winston the "Golden Country" of which he has often dreamed (he even encounters "a stream with green pools where dace were swimming," [816]), and the room over Mr. Charrington's shop, which Winston hires for their snatched meetings, is a recognizable echo of his past, with its enormous bed, like that of Winston's vanished mother, and its old-fashioned twelve-hour clock. The temporary safety of the love they share there is beautifully symbolized by the antique glass paperweight—"a little chunk of history they've forgotten to alter"—which Winston has bought from the apparently benign Charrington: "The paperweight was the room he was in, and the coral was Julia's life and his own, fixed in a sort of eternity at the heart of the crystal" (830).

The illusion of permanence, and the crystal itself (and thus the independent, solid past) are shattered at the end of part 2, when Winston and Julia are arrested, in a chilling scene that makes brutally clear the Party's total control and the primacy, in the world of *Nineteen Eighty-Four,* of physical fear over the power of love. Surrounded by the Thought Police, of whom Mr. Charrington is now seen to be one, there is no question of heroics for Winston, even when Julia is savagely punched in the stomach (870). From this point on, Julia vanishes from Winston's life (to reappear briefly in the last chapter, a brainwashed ghost like himself), and Winston exchanges the physical world, and all sense of time, for the closed, dialectical realm of O'Brien, the Inner

Party member with the "coarse, humorous brutal face" yet "a certain charm of manner," to whom Winston has been "deeply drawn" (748) from the beginning of the novel. This attraction, in fact, antedates Julia's by some years, and part 3, in revealing how all Winston's activities have been monitored, reveals also that the attraction has been mutual. The reasons for each man's interest in the other, however, are very different. Winston has thought of O'Brien as possibly a political dissident like himself; it is O'Brien for whom he writes the diary in which he has entered the axiom "Freedom is the freedom to say that two plus two make four" (790); and he has even dreamed of O'Brien's voice saying to him "We shall meet in the place where there is no darkness" (757). This "place" Winston sees as an "imagined future . . . which, by foreknowledge, one could mystically share in." It is, indeed, the future, but neither remote nor benign. Instead, it is the perpetually lit interrogation rooms of the Ministry of Love. There O'Brien, fiercely loyal to Ingsoc, and seeing Winston as an opponent worthy of his efforts, takes Winston through a grueling course of political reeducation, progressively enforced by beatings, hunger, electric shocks, argument, persuasion, and the final trial of Room 101 (one of Orwell's most memorable inventions in the novel, melodramatic perhaps but no less frightening), where individuals are confronted by whatever "worst thing in the world" (907) will reduce them to irreversible nonhumanity and so drive them into the loving arms of Big Brother, the deathless symbol of the impersonal omnipotent Party.

Winston's interrogation by O'Brien, too detailed to sum up adequately, and in its general gist too well-known to need repeating, answers a question Winston had asked the regime in part 1: "I understand HOW. I do not understand WHY" (789). Goldstein's book, which he receives from O'Brien in part 2 when he thinks him a member of the underground "Brotherhood," provides a full picture of the "how" of Ingsoc (its alteration of the past, its use of constant war to maintain physical and intellectual deprivation) in the two chapters that gloss the Party slogans "Ignorance is Strength" and "War is Peace." Winston does not, however, read chapter 2, presumably concerned with the third Party slogan "Freedom is Slavery." This is the "Why" of Ingsoc explained by O'Brien—one of the real authors of "the Book"—in part 3, chapter 3. The Party seeks power, not for the good of the people, but "entirely for its own sake"; that power is exercised in the infliction of "pain and humiliation," and Winston is invited (in an image repeated from *Coming Up for Air*) to envisage the future as "a boot stamping on a human face—for ever" (898). Power extends beyond the body to total control of the mind and thus of "reality": what the Party says is true, even if it be that two and two equal five. What is sanity and objectivity to Winston is to O'Brien mere mental derangement and "defective memory" (884). He is a minority of one, the "last man," holding out with remarkable courage against the Party's view—at times an insidious echo of religious dogma—that true freedom comes with the relinquishing of individuality. When Winston finally surrenders, it is in Room 101, where the threat of being eaten alive by rats causes him to scream "Do it to Julia!" (910), the ultimate disloyalty, which leaves him with nothing but Big Brother to fill the vacuum the months of indoctrination have created in him. The last pages of the novel, a year later than its opening, show the final flickerings of the old Winston—response to Julia, memories of his mother—dying into an acceptance of the system, a love of Big Brother, even a belief in the fictitious "victory" announced over the telescreen in the Chestnut Tree Café.

The relentless process that ends in Winston's reduction to little more than an automaton, beyond pity and therefore the more pitiable, is by turns fascinating and harrowing, according as one is caught up in the play of question and answer between Winston and O'Brien or emotionally involved in the plight of a victim of a system monstrous in its tyranny. It is an open question whether that system is too monstrous to be fully credible: Winston recognizes in O'Brien "a lunatic intensity" (889), perceptible not only in the latter's extreme pretensions to reality control, but in occasional contradictions between his statements. Nevertheless, this recognition does not eliminate Winston's fear of O'Brien, and the reader's doubt whether the world of *Nineteen Eighty-Four* could exist (that is, whether humanity as we still know it could cease to exist) is little protection against the experience created by its fictional expression, especially when Orwell so poignantly embodies, in Winston's memories and in his relationship with Julia, those aspects of decent human life that the existence of such a world would destroy.

This is not to say, however, that the force of *Nineteen Eighty-Four* resides essentially in its credibility as a political forecast or in its efficacy as a warning—even assuming such a "warning" could be effective. What accounts for its true power is its assembling, within an adequately credible fictional structure, of intensely felt human emotions: belief in decency (however "mystical"); fear of human evil and physical pain; response—strong as an ache—to natural beauty and vitality; nostalgia, sense of loss, love. There is, too, in the complex relationship of Winston and O'Brien (who at the end shades into Big Brother) another, and especially disturbing, reason for *Nineteen Eighty-Four*'s ability to haunt the mind even when the system it presents is discounted, a reason that places Winston as the extreme descendant of Flory, Comstock, even George Bowling. Winston fears O'Brien, eventually; but he continues to love him and to feel he is understood by him. O'Brien is "tormentor . . . protector . . . inquisitor . . . friend" (883). Winston's feelings are akin to the mingled fear and admiration sometimes felt by his victim for the school bully/hero,[33] and they are a reminder that the urge to dissent, to remain outside the system, to remain oneself, is often accompanied, or shadowed, by the need to conform, to belong, to be approved. Whether or not Orwell consciously realized the ambiguity, it is hard not to feel, in the ironic last words of *Nineteen Eighty-Four*—"He had won the victory over himself. He loved Big Brother"—an appeal to readers' understanding as well as to their sorrow.

Chapter Eight
"Farewell—and Hail"

On 17 April 1949, Easter Sunday, Orwell entered in the notebook he kept that year a short, Oscar Wilde–like aphorism: "At 50, everyone has the face he deserves."[1] Apart from a few letters to friends over the next six months, it was virtually the last thing Orwell wrote, and with a fine sense of the dramatic the editors of Orwell's *Collected Essays, Journalism and Letters* (1968) made it the final entry in their fourth volume. But what reads as a striking exit line was a verbal leap forward to an age, clearly deemed significant, that Orwell was not, in fact, to reach. He wrote it down in the private sanatorium in Gloucestershire to which his tuberculosis, exacerbated by the completion of *Nineteen Eighty-Four,* had sent him at the beginning of 1949; the face he displayed there was described by one of his visitors, Malcolm Muggeridge, as "like a thin sheet of fibre-glass with a furious furnace the other side."[2] In September, three months after his novel was published, Orwell was transferred to University College Hospital, London; here, the following month, he married Sonia Brownell, one of Cyril Connolly's editorial assistants at *Horizon.* Though unable to put on paper any of the writing projects that were in his head, he was cheerful and saw himself as slowly on the road to recovery. Instead, just before he was to have flown to a sanatorium in Switzerland, he died of a sudden lung hemorrhage on 21 January 1950. He was forty-six.

The instructions Orwell left for the disposal of his body,[3] carried out with the particular help of David Astor, whose influence obtained him a churchyard burial plot, had the effect, if not necessarily the intention, of returning him both to the Anglican church into which he had been confirmed at Eton, and to the identity that as an author he had chosen to discard. He was buried in the churchyard of All Saints Church, Sutton Courtenay—a quiet village on the Berkshire side of the Thames, forty miles upstream from the Shiplake of his boyhood. Over his grave, as he wished, is "a plain brown stone" inscribed "Here lies Eric Arthur Blair," and showing his dates of birth and death. No other information is given; whether Blair had wished, at last, to escape from Orwell, or Orwell from Blair, is an open question.

What remained, in 1950, were his books—six novels, three documentaries—together with a large quantity of miscellaneous journalism and essays, only a few of which had been collected in his lifetime. Haunted throughout his writing career by the feeling that he was "idling" and that his output was "miserably small,"[4] by 1949 (when he confided his views to his notebook) he had come to see it as "respectable." This, however, only made him fear that he "once had an industriousness and a fertility which I have now lost." The sense, here, of Orwell as a driven writer, unable to relax, is very strong; less obvious is his double view of writing as something that resulted both from natural talent and from hard work, even from a decision of the will. The effort he had begun in 1928, partly to become a writer, partly to justify his existence and perhaps, at first, to atone for his past, had never slackened; added to talent, indignation, an urge toward truth, and a distinct streak of independence verging on obstinacy, it produced by 1950 a body of work far from "miserably small." Given the partisan response that Orwell's work has a knack of producing, it is tempting to balance his own original underestimate by an equivalent overemphasis. But, in fact, Orwell's own correction, "respectable," is accurate enough when his output is compared with that of two exact contemporaries, Graham Greene and Evelyn Waugh. Both had written, by 1950, more novels than Orwell and about the same number of documentaries; if the total amount of Orwell's work gives him a slight edge on them, it is because of his many short pieces of nonfiction—the aspect of his work, incidentally, by which his identity of "George Orwell" was given its most directly recognizable expression in his lifetime. For, the contribution of Orwell to twentieth-century literature that most obviously differentiates him from his contemporaries is the projection, through his work, of a personality with which readers, whether or not they agree with what is said, can establish an immediate human connection. One of the shrewdest commentators on Orwell, Alex Zwerdling, has lucidly stated the relationship between Orwell and his work as one that leads, essentially, to a sense of "George Orwell" as something larger than the sum of his writings: "Nearly everything he wrote gives us the sense of a troubled consciousness attempting to find a means of expression that would serve all of his complex needs as an artist, as a political thinker, and as a human being.

It is perhaps our sense of the ambitiousness and inherent difficulty of this attempt that makes us discount some of the obvious imperfections of Orwell's work and see the career itself as more successful and impressive than the individual works it produced."[5]

Zwerdling, however, does not undervalue Orwell's actual books, which over the last thirty-five years have gone on gaining new readers and—especially since the spate of reprints, conferences, and discussions prompted by the arrival of the year 1984—show no sign of ceasing to do so. A new edition, and a manuscript facsimile, of *Nineteen Eighty-Four* have been published, Orwell's other books are being reedited, and the four-volume collection of his journalism, essays, and letters (1968) will eventually be supplanted by a much enlarged version. Such activities, together with the many studies of Orwell's work and the biographical explorations, which reached their fullest form in Bernard Crick's life of Orwell (1980), suggest the fascination posthumously exerted by Orwell as man and writer, and the wish (against his express request) to reconnect him with the Eric Blair out of whom he grew and who coexisted with him. On the pragmatic grounds stated by Orwell himself in "Lear, Tolstoy and the Fool"—that "there is no test of literary merit except survival"[6]—Orwell's survival so far argues the high quality of his work.

Early posthumous responses to Orwell sometimes had a touch of the hagiographic—understandable reflections, perhaps, of the known austerity of his life and the earliness of his death. Writing his obituary for the *New Statesman,* V. S. Pritchett even referred to him as "a kind of saint,"[7] something Orwell would not have appreciated in view of his own opening phrase in "Reflections on Gandhi," his last essay published just a year earlier: "Saints should always be judged guilty until they are proved innocent."[8] Yet a quasi-official view of Orwell as something close to a saint can be discerned in the popular magazine *Picture Post,* which published not long after his death a group of photographs taken in London in 1946 by two Anarchist friends, Vernon Richards and his wife, Marie Louise Berneri, who were associated with the Freedom Press. One of these, showing the tall, lined face with sunken eyes and toothbrush moustache, which in the last four decades has become rather too familiar a cultural icon, bears the caption: "Here, Orwell drinks strong, sweet tea and smokes a black self-rolled cigarette: two of the few weaknesses he permitted himself."[9] After the editorial smarminess of this, it is a relief to turn to a letter from Orwell to Richards, written in summer 1949 from the sanatorium at Cranham in Gloucestershire, and hear in obvious response to a request about these very photographs the casual practicality of a real human being: "Sell as many photos as you can. It doesn't cost *me* anything, and it is all advertisement."[10] For Orwell, the "advertisement" was for his books, not for himself.

More apposite, more lasting, and more relevant to Orwell's books was the remark with which V. S. Pritchett began his obituary: Orwell was "the wintry conscience of a generation which in the thirties had heard the call to the rasher assumptions of political faith."[11] Over the years this has often been quoted, though usually in an abbreviated form: "Orwell was the wintry conscience of his generation." This, by widening the context, distorts Pritchett's meaning. But in either formulation it is the words "wintry" and "conscience" that stand out, claiming for Orwell a degree of moral integrity and mental independence that makes him special among his contemporaries. That his physical face has become the most instantly recognizable of any British writer of his generation is intimately linked with the ability of his authorial voice to summon readers into his concerns, to persuade them to agree, or to defy them not to.

A response to this dialectical summons marked Orwell's earliest book-length critics—John Atkins and Laurence Brander in 1954, Christopher Hollis two years later. All three had known him personally, and drew out of his work for close inspection the ideas and attitudes by which it was animated. For Atkins, "the common element in all George Orwell's writings was a sense of decency"; for Brander, Orwell was a "born writer" who "concentrated his energies on making people more conscious of [the] danger" of totalitarianism.[12] Neither critic, though admiring, was content with a slavish demonstration of Orwell's views; both paid his work the compliment of intelligent, though not academic, discussion and, occasionally, dissent. Christopher Hollis went one stage further. An Etonian contemporary of Orwell, he was able to look more critically at Orwell's presentation of his early life and schooling, and, because of this, to evaluate—or at least to question—the objectivity of many of Orwell's attitudes to the world. Hollis also, as a Roman Catholic and a Conservative Member of Parliament, brought a different, but by no means bigoted, political perspective to bear on Orwell's, and sensed in his agnosticism at least a leaning toward religious belief. All this may suggest an approach to Orwell that is debunking or at best irrelevant; in fact Hollis's study is both searching and essentially sympathetic, as its single-sentence final paragraph eloquently demonstrates: "Whatever judgement may be passed on this or that detail of his arguments no one can challenge the final verdict on Orwell that in an age when all good things were desperately assaulted by tyrants of so many sorts and when so many at one time or another belittled the dangers on the one flank in order to concentrate on the dangers of the other, he almost alone from first to last dealt out his blows impartially and defended without fear and without compromise the cause of liberty and the decencies from whatever quarter they might be assailed."[13]

"This was the noblest Roman of them all" Hollis might almost have been saying. His remarks exemplify the perception of Orwell's work—*Animal Farm, Nineteen Eighty-Four,* his documentaries, many of his essays, and less obviously his prewar novels—as having a humanitarian and, in the broadest sense, a political "message." This aspect of Orwell has continued to attract commentators, in England the more so as tertiary education has, since Orwell's death, given an increasingly powerful voice, in journalism and academic criticism, to members of the working class whose way of life he described and to some extent shared. For some of them, perhaps, an admiration for Orwell is in part self-vindication, in part a form of nostalgia for a life-style they have moved away from; though the working-class critic may also feel that Orwell shared with the 1930s "Nancy poets" he derided a habit of "slumming" and an outsider's "pastoral" view of the proletariat. Recent feminist critics—most notably Daphne Patai in the United States[14]—have certainly objected to Orwell's view of women, who, however sympathetically they may be presented, play no more than a sexual and/or domestic role in his work. Such a reductive portrayal constitutes, for Patai, a disabling flaw in Orwell's human awareness and concern for fair play; that it can also seriously weaken his literary responsiveness is indicated by his summary, in a 1943 radio broadcast on *Macbeth,* of the "theme" of *Antony and Cleopatra* as "the power which a worthless woman can establish over a brave and gifted man."[15] While admitting the abstract justice of Patai's point, one may defend Orwell as merely a child of his generation, intending no harm and unaware of prejudice. Yet it is precisely Orwell's keenness to question and expose so many other assumptions of his time that makes his own blind acceptance of this one—"One sex is more equal than the other"—harder to exonerate.

"Message," however—whether this subliminal one or the many others presented with full consciousness throughout his work—is only one part of Orwell. Its presence has done much to keep his name alive, and to distinguish him from literary contemporaries with less itchy polemical trigger fingers and longer imaginative fuses. Raymond Williams, at the end of his short study of Orwell published in 1971, fairly prophesied that "We are never likely to reach a time when we can do without his frankness, his energy, his willingness to join in."[16] And yet, foolish as Joseph II's famous remark—"Too many notes, Herr Mozart"—may have been, one is sometimes tempted to echo him with "Too many opinions, Mr. Orwell." It may be true—to quote an opinion expressed in "Politics and the English Language"—that "the great enemy of clear language is insincerity";[17] at the same time, sincerity is not always enough, and opinions do not necessarily assemble into a clear system. As a recent commentator on Orwell's ideas, Ian Slater, points out, Orwell "is a better social critic than he is a political thinker. Although we always know unequivocally what he is *against,* we are never as certain about what he was *for.*"[18] But, as Slater admits, "as a novelist and journalist," Orwell's task was not to provide "remedies for society's ills." Particularly since the mid-1960s, there have been critics who have wanted, while not ignoring "message," to draw attention to "medium," especially Orwell's use of the medium of fiction.

Much, for instance, of George Woodcock's study *The Crystal Spirit* (1966)—still, perhaps, the most acute and comprehensive single study of Orwell—is concerned with elements in his work that are the product not of a wish to influence the reader's thinking but of that "aesthetic enthusiasm" that Orwell listed in "Why I Write" as one of the four ingredients of the impulse to authorship.[19] Woodcock brings out particularly well the vividness of Orwell's descriptive writing, notably his lyrical descriptions of jungle landscape in *Burmese Days,* including the pool in which Flory bathes (chap. 4), gaining a temporary feeling of peace. With its "baptismal implications," the pool is a natural symbol;[20] as, to very different effect, is the aspidistra in Orwell's third novel. Woodcock also notes the recurrence in Orwell's novels of various motifs, especially the use of imagery derived from animals and relating human beings to them: *Animal Farm* can thus be seen not simply as an isolated animal fable but as a book that adopts in extenso a characteristic way of seeing the world. This delineation of symbol and significant motif, only one aspect of Woodcock's study, became the informing principle of the first book on Orwell to originate in the United States, and the first to be devoted (with the exception of a section on *Homage to Catalonia,* seen as a turning point) to Orwell's novels. In *Orwell's*

Fiction (1969), Robert A. Lee analyzes Orwell's use of natural/animal imagery in *Burmese Days,* the frequent occurrence in his work of churches, the pervasiveness, in *Nineteen-Eighty-Four,* of dust and, throughout his fiction, of protagonists who are in some way "wounded." Though not always plausible in its details, Lee's study has the merit of suggesting that Orwell's novels are not just the products of, in Keats's term, "palpable design," but also communicate at a deeper level, as fiction should. It is not easy, however, to agree with Lee's final assessment that Orwell rates, as a novelist, with E. M. Forster, an altogether subtler user of the medium. A later study, Alex Zwerdling's *Orwell and the Left* (1974), suggests why Orwell is the lesser novelist. While granting that Orwell's novels are "regularly symbolic," Zwerdling finds that their symbols "rarely kindle into life"—not so much because they could not as because Orwell, fearing their misrepresentation by the reader, will not leave them free to do so: "One constantly feels that Orwell thought of the novel as a kind of monster which could feel but not think, and onto which he was determined to graft a brain—his own."[21]

Irritation at Orwell's frequent authorial intrusions, at least in the prewar novels, springs to mind in support of Zwerdling's painstakingly argued position; yet, as Woodcock points out, Orwell's "polemical arguments, even when they occur in the wrong places, are always intensely readable,"[22] and Zwerdling himself clearly sees Orwell's dilemma as an honorable one, the result of his difficult attempt to weld together—or fulfill in the same book—political and aesthetic purposes. Laurence Brander, twenty years earlier, had expressed more or less Zwerdling's view, but in rather different terms: "If Orwell had lived to forget to be didactic, we should have had a fine novelist."[23]

That he might have do so, having fused didactic intention with fictional form remarkably well in the two "special case" novels *Animal Farm* and *Nineteen Eighty-Four,* is suggested by a letter he wrote to his friend Tosco Fyvel in the spring of 1949. There he mentioned having "in my head . . . a novel dealing with 1945"—that is, one may reasonably infer, a novel of the realistic sort he had published in the 1930s. Then, however, he had "sometimes written a so-called novel within about two years of the original conception, but . . . they were always weak, silly books which I afterwards suppressed"—a clear reference to *A Clergyman's Daughter* and *Keep the Aspidistra Flying.* Now, though, he was determined to allow more of what I have earlier referred to as "assimilation time" to pass before he began writing: "even if I survive to write it I shouldn't touch it before 1950," because "a novel has to be lived with for years before it can be written down, otherwise the working-out of detail . . . can't happen."[24] Orwell's letter suggests two things: a willingness not to hurry the workings of his fictional imagination, and that, having issued his warning about the future—which Bernard Crick has very sensibly called "not his *summa* . . . [but] the last great book he happened to write before he happened to die"[25]—he felt more able to face the realities of the present.

Other evidence points to a wish not only to turn back to realistic fiction, but back to the past. In December 1948, just before he left Jura, he informed Fredric Warburg that he had "a stunning idea for a very short novel which has been in my head for years."[26] This is unlikely to have been the "1945" novel, judging from part of a conversation noted down by Warburg after a visit six months later to the sanatorium at Cranham. "I asked him about a novel, and this is formulated in his mind—a nouvelle of 30,000 to 40,000 words—a novel of character rather than ideas, with Burma as background."[27] The loss of this contemplated novel is particularly hard, not only because, in treating place and character, it might have benefited from the objectivity Orwell had begun to practice in the 1940s, but because it might have brought Orwell's career full circle back to the country that compelled his earliest fictional imaginings as Eric Blair, and shown how George Orwell, twenty-five years later, had come to see it.

But Orwell never reached fifty, and "the face he deserves" is to be made out from the books he actually wrote. By general consent, two are preeminent and would by themselves ensure Orwell the stature of a minor master: *Animal Farm,* compressed, resonantly simple, the product of the "struggle to efface one's own personality" that Orwell, late, had come to value, and written in the "prose like a window pane"[28] that has come to seem his peculiar property; and *Nineteen Eighty-Four,* with its claustrophobic ability to involve readers in the details of its world even when (as Orwell might have hoped) they disagree with the assumptions behind it. More and more, also, *Homage to Catalonia* is seen as the forerunner of, and runner-up to, those books, not only in laying the groundwork for their fictional visions, but in showing Orwell's ability to marshal complex material with lucidity and confidence.

The prewar novels, though less satisfactory as total structures and frequently intruded on by authorial comment and polemic, nevertheless continue to repay reading by the vividness with which they reproduce the texture of unprivileged human life and the pressures of the period in which they are set. As much as anything else, they are involving historical records, most obviously of imperial Burma and Edwardian England, but also of various forms of provincial life in the interwar years. They communicate deprivation, frustration, and indignation with especial immediacy, and may have had some influence thereby on the new generation, and class, of novelists who emerged in England a few years after Orwell's death. One recognizes in some of the protagonists of Kingsley Amis and John Wain (particularly Charles Lumley in the latter's *Hurry on Down* [1953]) the heroes of early Orwell, and in the down-to-earth realism of their depictions of life beneath the harrow an echo of the openings of *Keep the Aspidistra Flying* and *Coming Up for Air.*

His availability as an influence on the new writers of the 1950s indicates two aspects of Orwell whose coexistence points to what is perhaps the central element in his life and work. Vigilant, independent, quick to question social injustice, and concerned to warn against what he saw as society's movement toward regimentation, Orwell's writings can well be characterized by the phrase "I rebel, therefore I am." It is an appropriate label, in view of his choice of a life-style so divergent from those of his literary contemporaries that it is difficult to find common ground for comparison between him and them. At the same time—and because, perhaps, of that very divergence, which began by the avoidance of university and led to an awareness of the lives first of underdogs and then of ordinary people—he was technically an old-fashioned writer, content with realistic modes and linear presentation, whose tastes were for the famous authors of the past and for a range of more modern works, which could be labeled "middlebrow." As John Atkins pointed out in 1954, there was "nothing *avant-garde* about Orwell"[29]—except his emulation of James Joyce in one section of *A Clergyman's Daughter.* If he was a "revolutionary," as Cyril Connolly and George Woodcock both called him, Orwell was also "a revolutionary who is in love with 1910."[30] Even his attitude to language, stated most explicitly in his essay "Politics and the English Language" and in the appendix on "Newspeak" in *Nineteen Eighty-Four,* can be categorized, as W. F. Bolton in a recent linguistic study has suggested, as a form of "nostalgia."[31]

Rightly or wrongly, Orwell located his virtues of decency and "comeliness" in the era in which, only imperfectly knowing it, he grew up, and together with his concern that society remain worth living in, it is his belief that it had once been so that accounts for an enduring aspect of his appeal. John Atkins, claiming "uniqueness" for Orwell among twentieth-century writers, located his special quality in the fact that he combined "the mind of an intellectual with the feelings of a common man."[32] Given Orwell's tendency to the instinctive rather than to the systematic, he might better be defined as the ordinary person's idea of an intellectual, an identity that, considering his hostility to the inhumane remoteness of theoreticians, he might not have thought reductive. Stark and memorable, naive yet compelling, the words Orwell gave Winston Smith, to define his existence against the enveloping darkness of Ingsoc, powerfully express the common sense of the past as the enduring truth of the present: "The obvious, the silly and the true had got to be defended. Truisms are true, hold on to that! The solid world exists, its laws do not change, stones are hard, water is wet, objects unsupported fall toward the earth's centre" (790).

Notes and References

Chapter One

1. Jacintha Buddicom, *Eric and Us: A Remembrance of George Orwell* (London: Leslie Frewin, 1974), 11.

2. *The Road to Wigan Pier,* Penguin Complete Longer Non-Fiction of George Orwell (Harmondsworth, England: Penguin Books, 1983), 230. Further references follow in the text.

3. See Bernard Crick, *George Orwell: A Life* (1980; reprint ed., Harmondsworth, England: Penguin Books, 1982), 59.

4. *Keep the Aspidistra Flying,* Penguin Complete Novels of George Orwell (Harmondsworth, England: Penguin Books, 1983), 601. Further references follow in the text.

5. The school was near the concentration of army barracks at Aldershot, and a great many of its pupils went on to Sandhurst and officers' commissions.

6. Orwell, "Such, Such Were the Joys," in *Collected Essays, Journalism and Letters of George Orwell,* ed. Sonia Orwell and Ian Angus, 4 vols. (1968; reprint ed., Harmondsworth, England: Penguin Books, 1970), 4:416.

7. It was first published after Orwell's death, with a slightly truncated ending, in *Partisan Review* 19, no. 5 (September-October 1952). The original, full version appears in *Collected Essays,* ed. Orwell and Angus, 4:379–422.

8. Cyril Connolly, *Enemies of Promise* (London: Routledge & Kegan Paul, 1938; reprinted., Harmondsworth, England: Penguin Books, 1961). Chapter 19, "White Samite," deals with St. Cyprian's under the name "St. Wulfric's."

9. See Crick, *Life,* 68–70.

10. Connolly, *Enemies of Promise,* 177.

11. A very penetrating discussion of this matter occurs in T. R. Fyvel, *George Orwell: A Personal Memoir* (1982; reprint ed., London: Hutchinson, 1983), 16–30.

12. It is fair to mention, however, that Blair's contemporary and friend Jacintha Buddicom, who knew him well from 1914 onwards, deals trenchantly with his complaints in *Eric and Us,* 45–56.

13. Letter to Ida Blair, 8 December 1912. Blair's letters to his mother are housed with the many other Orwell papers in the Orwell Archive at University College, London.

14. Letter to Ida Blair, 3 March 1912, Orwell Archive, University College, London.

15. *Election* is the Eton term for the group of King's Scholars admitted each year. Henry VI's original foundation provided for a total of seventy spread over the five school years.

16. Crick, *Life,* 101.

17. Denys King-Farlow, "Eton Days with George Orwell," in *Orwell Remembered,* ed. Audrey Coppard and Bernard Crick. (London: British Broadcasting Corporation, 1984), 55.

18. Connolly, *Enemies of Promise,* 204.

19. Orwell, "For Ever Eton," *Observer,* 1 August 1948.

20. Crick, *Life,* 122.

21. Denys King-Farlow, "Eton Days," 57.

22. Quoted in Crick, *Life,* 105.

23. Steven Runciman, "A Contemporary in College," in *Orwell Remembered,* 51.

24. Quoted by Christopher Hollis, "Orwell at Eton," in *Orwell Remembered,* 43.

25. Ibid. The Officer Training Corps (or Cadet Force) was a standard feature of public school life in Britain for many years, usually involving compulsory membership.

26. Denys King-Farlow, BBC broadcast, 1960, quoted in Crick, *Life,* 102.

27. Runciman, "A Contemporary," 52.

28. In conversation with the writer, August 1984.

29. King-Farlow, "Eton Days," 57.

30. Hollis, "Orwell at Eton," 42.

31. Letter to Steven Runciman, August 1920, in *Collected Essays,* ed. Orwell and Angus, 1:34.

32. Buddicom, *Eric and Us,* 76.

33. Ibid., 41.

34. See David Pryce-Jones, *Cyril Connolly: Journal and Memoir* (London: Collins, 1983), 44.

35. Buddicom, *Eric and Us,* 117.

36. Ibid., 152.

37. Ibid., 77.

38. Fyvel, *George Orwell,* 36.

39. Runciman, "A Contemporary," 52.

40. Roger Beadon, quoted in Crick, *Life,* 148.

41. Maung Htin Aung, "George Orwell and Burma," in *The World of George Orwell,* ed. Miriam Gross (London: Weidenfeld & Nicolson, 1971), 24.

42. Crick, *Life,* 167.

43. Buddicom, *Eric and Us,* 143.

44. "A Hanging," in *Collected Essays,* ed. Orwell and Angus, 1:68.

45. "Shooting an Elephant," in *Collected Essays,* ed. Orwell and Angus, 1:272.

46. Ibid., 269.
47. In *Le Progrès civique,* 4 May 1929, quoted in Crick, *Life,* 173.
48. Crick, *Life,* 169.
49. "Why I Write," in *Collected Essays,* ed. Orwell and Angus, 1:23.

Chapter Two

1. See Crick, *Life,* 195–96.
2. Robert Frost, "The Death of the Hired Man," in *The Poetry of Robert Frost,* ed. Edwin Connery Latham. (London: Jonathan Cape, 1971), 38.
3. Ruth Pitter, in *Orwell Remembered,* 69–70.
4. *Down and Out in Paris and London,* Non-Fiction (Harmondsworth, England: Penguin Books, 1983), 6. Further references follow in the text.
5. Quoted in Crick, *Life,* 188.
6. Letter from L. I. Bailey to Eric Blair, 23 April 1929, quoted in Crick, *Life,* 194.
7. Review of *Angel Pavement* by J. B. Priestley, in *Collected Essays,* ed. Orwell and Angus, 1:49.
8. Crick, *Life,* 214.
9. Ibid., 219.
10. Letters to Leonard Moore, 6 July and 19 November 1932, in *Collected Essays,* ed. Orwell and Angus, 1:108, 132.
11. Letter to Leonard Moore, 26 April 1932, in ibid., 101.
12. Letter to Leonard Moore, 9 July 1932, in ibid., 108.
13. Letter to Leonard Moore, 19 November 1932, in ibid., 131.
14. Crick, *Life,* 235.
15. Quoted in Crick, *Life,* 236.
16. W. H. Davies, review of *Down and Out in Paris and London, New Statesman and Nation,* 18 March 1933, quoted in *George Orwell: The Critical Heritage,* ed. Jeffrey Meyers (London and Boston: Routledge & Kegan Paul, 1975), 44.
17. Ernest Dowson, "Villanelle of the Poet's Road," as usually quoted. (Dowson actually wrote "Wine and woman and song.")
18. See letters to Leonard Moore, 1 July 1932 and 6 July 1932, in *Collected Essays,* ed. Orwell and Angus, 1:107–8.
19. Crick, *Life,* 225.
20. Orwell, Introduction to the French edition (1935), reprinted in *Collected Essays,* ed. Orwell and Angus, 1:138.
21. See *Collected Essays,* ed. Orwell and Angus, 1:139–41.
22. Crick, *Life,* 223.
23. Letter to Henry Miller, 26 August, 1936, in *Collected Essays,* ed. Orwell and Angus, 1:259.
24. Letter to Leonard Moore, 1 July 1932, in ibid., 108.

25. Christopher Sykes, *New Republic,* 4 December 1950, 30–31, reprinted in *George Orwell,* ed. Meyers, 309.

26. Crick, *Life,* 213.

27. Letter to Eleanor Jaques, 19 October 1932, in *Collected Essays,* ed. Orwell and Angus, 1:28.

28. Letter to Leonard Moore, 1 February 1933, in ibid., 139.

29. Letter to Brenda Salkeld, 10 [?] December 1933, in ibid., 153.

30. Letter to Brenda Salkeld, August 1934, in ibid., 162.

31. Cyril Connolly, review of *Burmese Days, New Statesman and Nation,* 6 July 1935, 18–20; the Gorer passage is quoted in Crick, *Life,* 264; G. W. Stonier, review of *Burmese Days, Fortnightly,* August 1935, 255, reprinted in *George Orwell,* ed. Meyers, 53.

32. Letter to Henry Miller, 27 August 1936, in *Collected Essays,* ed. Orwell and Angus, 1:258.

33. Cf. a remark from the manuscript notebook Orwell kept during the last year of his life: "even in a novel the author must occasionally comment." *Collected Essays,* ed. Orwell and Angus, 48:575.

34. "Why I Write," in *Collected Essays;* ed. Orwell and Angus, 1:25.

35. Ibid., 1:30.

36. *Burmese Days,* Penguin Complete Novels of George Orwell (Harmondsworth, England: Penguin Books, 1983). Further references follow in the text.

37. "Why I Write," in *Collected Essays,* ed. Orwell and Angus, 1:30.

38. The novel's motif of a white man who loses his chance of happiness with a white woman through her discovery of an earlier liaison with a native girl resembles Maugham's short story "The Force of Circumstance," set in Borneo.

39. Letter to Leonard Moore, 8 February 1934, in *Collected Essays,* ed. Orwell and Angus, 1:158. In view of Orwell's early disparagement of Priestley, it is amusing to note that such a "tying up" chapter concludes *The Good Companions* (1929).

Chapter Three

1. L. P. Hartley, review of *A Clergyman's Daughter, Observer,* 10 March 1935, 6.

2. Peter Quennell, review of *A Clergyman's Daughter, New Statesman and Nation,* 23 March 1935, 421–22.

3. Letter to Leonard Moore, 3 October 1934, in *Collected Essays,* ed. Orwell and Angus, 1:165.

4. On the latter, see Crick, *Life,* 246.

5. Letter to Brenda Salkeld, 7 March 1935, in *Collected Essays,* ed. Orwell and Angus, 1:174.

6. Letter to Henry Miller, 26 August 1936, in ibid. 258.

7. *A Clergyman's Daughter,* (Harmondsworth, England: Penguin Books, 1983), 423. Further references follow in the text.

8. Letter to Eleanor Jaques, 14[?] June 1932, in *Collected Essays,* ed. Orwell and Angus, 1:105.

9. Crick, *Life,* 226. (As the local church was "High," the service was called "Mass," in Roman Catholic fashion.)

10. Letter to Eleanor Jaques, 14[?] June 1932, in *Collected Essays,* ed. Orwell and Angus, 1:106.

11. Review of *The Spirit of Catholicism* by Karl Adam, in *New English Weekly,* 9 June 1932, Orwell and Angus, 1:102–5.

12. Letter to Eleanor Jaques, 19 September 1932, in ibid., 127.

13. Brenda Salkeld, "He Didn't Really Like Women," in *Orwell Remembered,* 67.

14. Hartley, review, 6.

15. "Why I Write," in *Penguin Essays,* 10.

16. While in Hayes, Orwell had himself sat behind such a woman at a communion service.

17. *Coming Up for Air* (Harmondsworth, England: Penguin Books, 1983), pt. 4, chap. 6. Further references follow in the text.

18. He does, in fact, speak of "a change in the climate of the mind," but not until chap. 4 (398).

19. Letter to Brenda Salkeld, 7 March 1935, in *Collected Essays,* ed. Orwell and Angus, 1:174.

20. V. S. Pritchett, review of *A Clergyman's Daughter, Spectator,* 22 March 1935, 504.

21. A conflation of the real London suburbs Uxbridge and Southall (near Hayes).

22. See especially 392–93.

23. A very close parallel to this phrase occurs in Aldous Huxley's *Crome Yellow* (1921), chap. 6. One of the "inspired" aphorisms of the journalist Mr. Barbecue-Smith runs: "The Things that Really Matter happen in the Heart."

24. Gracie Fields lived from 1898 to 1979, and was made a Dame of the Order of the British Empire shortly before her death.

25. Letter to Brenda Salkeld, 16 February 1935, in *Collected Essays,* ed. Orwell and Angus, 1:172.

26. Letter to Rayner Heppenstall, September 1935, in ibid., 176.

27. Letter to George Woodcock, 28 September 1946, in ibid., 4:241.

28. Louis Simpson, review of *Keep the Aspidistra Flying, Hudson Review,* 9, no. 2 Summer 1956, 306–7.

29. The poem (signed "Eric Blair") was called "On a Ruined Farm near the His Majesty's Voice Gramophone Factory," in *Collected Essays,* ed. Orwell and Angus, 1:158–59.

30. See Crick, *Life,* 231.

31. See Kay Ekevall, "Hampstead Friendship," in *Orwell Remembered,*

101. Kay Ekevall was one of his girlfriends when he worked in Hampstead; but her statement that, after the meal, he "assaulted a policeman" is not confirmed in Crick's biography.

32. "Bookshop Memories," *Fortnightly,* November 1936, in *Collected Essays,* ed. Orwell and Angus, 1:272–77.

33. Entry in *Collins's Dictionary of the English Language* (1979).

34. Orwell used to attend literary parties at the home of the old 1890s poet T. Sturge Moore; he refused invitations from the Scottish (Orkney) poet Edwin Muir.

35. One must make allowances for history here: one notes that, when Rosemary and Comstock marry, both assume she will give up her job.

36. The use of an advertising agency in the novel may owe something to *Murder Must Advertise* (1928) by Dorothy L. Sayers, which in the intervals of its detective story plot has much to say, though more lightly, about the cynical exploitation involved in advertising and the pressures of inadequate income on some of those who work at "Pym's Publicity." (One of the characters in that novel is called "Mr. Tallboy"—cf. "Mr. Tallboys" in *A Clergyman's Daughter.*) Orwell reviewed Dorothy Sayers's novel *Gaudy Night* in the *New English Weekly,* 23 January 1936, in *Collected Essays,* ed. Orwell and Angus, 1:185–86.

37. Cyril Connolly, review of *Keep the Aspidistra Flying, New Statesman and Nation,* 25 April 1936, 635.

38. Dorothy van Ghent, review of *Keep the Aspidistra Flying, Yale Review* 45, no. 3 (March 1956), 463.

39. Letter to Jack Common, 16 February 1938, in *Collected Essays,* ed. Orwell and Angus, 1:396.

40. See letter to John Sceats, 26 October 1938, in ibid., 396. Orwell had written to Sceats, an insurance agent, for "correct" details that he could use in his presentation of Bowling's professional life. He described Bowling as living in "a suburb which might be Hayes or Southall."

41. "On a Ruined Farm . . . ," *Adelphi,* April 1934, in *Collected Essays,* ed. Orwell and Angus, 1:158–59.

42. Crick, *Life,* 359.

43. Quoted in Crick, *Life,* 370.

44. "Marrakech," *New Writing,* Spring 1939.

45. Letter to Cyril Connolly, 14 December 1938, in *Collected Essays,* ed. Orwell and Angus, 1:400.

46. Letter to Julian Symons, 10 May 1948, in ibid., 4:478.

47. Review of *Coming Up for Air, Times Literary Supplement,* 17 June 1939, 355.

48. "Inside the Whale," in Penguin Essays, 115.

49. In ibid., 207.

50. Letter to Julian Symons, 10 May 1948, in *Collected Essays,* ed. Orwell and Angus, 4:478.

51. Printed in ibid., 574–75.

52. Orwell does not mention *Coming Up for Air* in these notes; but given his habit of changing his views about earlier work, it seems reasonable to assume that his opinions of the first-person novel are at least partly derived from his own single exercise in this form.

53. Crick, *Life,* 376.

54. Perhaps the "in general" is intended as a large escape clause; though if it is, it reduces Orwell's statement to meaninglessness. If not, one wonders what meaning and value Orwell attached to the term "true novel" if it had to exclude *Tristram Shandy, Great Expectations,* and *A la recherche du temps perdu.*

55. Christopher Hollis wrote that the two (adult) singers were a transposed recollection of two loud choir members (nicknamed "Thunderguts" and "Rumbletummy") in Eton College Chapel when Orwell was at Eton. (See Hollis, *A Study of George Orwell* [London: Hollis & Carter, 1956], 110.)

56. Orwell's place name is clearly meant, however, to suggest the area in which he was brought up. There is a tiny hamlet called Binfield Heath two miles west of Shiplake, and "Binfeild [*sic*] Hundred" was in the seventeenth century one of the administrative divisions ("hundreds") of Oxfordshire, covering an area that included Shiplake and Henley.

Chapter Four

1. W. H. Auden, "Spain" (1937).

2. "Why I Write," in *Collected Essays,* ed. Orwell and Angus, 1:28.

3. Bernard Crick notes that "Orwell told Geoffrey Gorer that but for the money he would never have gone." *Life,* 278.

4. Listed in "Why I Write" first among authorial motives.

5. "'The Road to Wigan Pier' Diary," in *Collected Essays,* ed. Orwell and Angus, 1:218.

6. Four pieces, by Humphrey Dakin, Joe ("Jerry") Kennan, Mary Deiner, and Sydney Smith, which appear in *Orwell Remembered,* 127–39.

7. See *Collected Essays,* ed. Orwell and Angus, 1:194–243.

8. Crick, *Life,* 278.

9. It was in Wigan. In the "Diary" (perhaps confusing its name with that of the famous murderer) Orwell called it "Crippen's Mine" (210); Jerry Kennan, who arranged Orwell's visit, called it "Cribbens" (quoted in Crick, *Life,* 284).

10. The ability of some critics to misread Orwell is pointed up sharply in connection with this passage. Reviewing *Wigan Pier* on its appearance in the United States in 1958, Robert Hatch referred to it as describing "malformed miners." (See *George Orwell,* ed. Meyers, 114.)

11. "Diary," 210.

12. In Barnsley he attended a meeting addressed by the Fascist (Blackshirt) leader Sir Oswald Mosley. ("Diary," 230–32.)

13. Walter Greenwood (1904–1974), review of *The Road to Wigan Pier, Tribune,* 12 March 1937, reprinted in *George Orwell,* ed. Meyers, 99–100.

14. Letter to Jack Common, 5 October 1936, in *Collected Essays,* ed. Orwell and Angus, 1:263.

15. J. B. Priestley, *English Journey* (1934; Jubilee reprint ed., London: Heinemann, 1984), 260.

16. This was not Orwell's fault: he had not been asked to take photographs. But the illustrations, relating to east London, South Wales, the Northeast, and Scotland, caused Walter Greenwood in his review to assume that Orwell had been to all these places on his "tour."

17. "Diary," 203.

18. Victor Gollancz, Foreword to *The Road to Wigan Pier* (1937), reprinted in *George Orwell,* ed. Meyers, 91–99.

19. H. J. Laski, review of *The Road to Wigan Pier, Left News,* March 1937, 275–76.

20. See "With the Wigan Miners," an interview with Jerry Kennan in *Orwell Remembered,* 130–33.

21. *Homage to Catalonia* (Harmondsworth, England: Penguin Books, 1983), 379. Further references follow in the text.

22. Crick, *Life,* 311–12.

23. Not his only one. The *New Statesman* had refused to publish his essay "Spilling the Spanish Beans" and his review of Franz Borkenau's *The Spanish Cockpit.* Both were written before he started *Homage to Catalonia.* (See Crick, *Life,* 340–41.)

24. Hugh Thomas, *The Spanish Civil War* (1961; reprint ed., Harmondsworth, England: Pelican Books, 1968), 544 n. A small but significant instance of Orwell's inaccuracy about details occurs in chap. 13, where he refers to a male "Federico Montsenys, an ex-member of the Government" (*Homage,* 449), instead of the female Frederica Montseny (Minister of Health in the central government led by Largo Caballero).

25. Letter to Jack Common, 5 February 1938, in *Collected Essays,* ed. Orwell and Angus, 1:330.

26. "Looking Back on the Spanish War," in *Penguin Complete Longer Non-Fiction,* (Harmondsworth, England: Penguin Books, 1983), 488. The last phrase was used by George Woodcock as the title of his book on Orwell.

27. Crick, *Life,* 318.

28. Letter to Cyril Connolly, 8 July 1938, in *Collected Essays,* ed. Orwell and Angus, 1:380.

29. Thomas, *Spanish Civil War,* 772.

Chapter Five

1. Letter to Geoffrey Gorer, 20 January 1939, in *Collected Essays,* ed. Orwell and Angus, 1:421.

2. In ibid., 2:39; autobiographical note published in *Twentieth Century Authors,* ed. Stanley Kunitz and H. Haycraft (New York: H. W. Wilson Co., 1942).

3. Letter to Geoffrey Gorer, 10 January 1940, in *Collected Essays,* ed. Orwell and Angus, 1:450.

4. Crick, *Life,* 387–88.

5. *The Lion and the Unicorn,* in *Penguin Essays,* 191.

6. Letter to A. S. F. Gow, 13 April 1946, in *Collected Essays,* ed. Orwell and Angus, 4:178.

7. Reprinted in ibid., 2:153–57 and 229–40.

8. Crick, *Life,* 482.

9. Ibid., 467.

10. "Why I Write," in *Penguin Essays,* 11.

11. E. M. Forster, *Listener,* 2 November 1950, reprinted in *George Orwell,* ed. Meyers, 304.

12. Published in the United States under the title "Such, Such Were the Joys."

13. The title of this essay may be modeled on "How the Poor Live," a long piece (110 pages) of serious reporting by George R. Sims (1847–1922). (London: Chatto & Windus, 1889.)

14. A longer treatment of literature for boys, in which Orwell's essay "Boys' Weeklies" is mentioned (chap. 13), is E. S. Turner's *Boys Will Be Boys* (London: Michael Joseph, 1948).

15. "Boys' Weeklies," in *Penguin Essays,* 106. Further references to essays discussed in this chapter will be to this edition and will follow in the text.

16. Crick, *Life,* 502–3.

17. The notion was extended in 1945 in Orwell's short essay in *Tribune,* "Good Bad Books"—a term originally coined by G. K. Chesterton.

18. It was to have appeared in the *Saturday Book* (London: Hutchinson, 1944).

Chapter Six

1. "Arthur Koestler," in *Penguin Essays,* 274.

2. Letter to Gleb Struve, 17 February 1944, in *Collected Essays,* ed. Orwell and Angus, 3:118–19.

3. "Why I Write," in *Penguin Essays,* 12.

4. Crick, *Life,* 487.

5. In *Collected Essays,* ed. Orwell and Angus, 3:458.

6. Ibid., 459.

7. A disenchanted view of the wartime Russophile attitude in Britain is apparent in Evelyn Waugh's *Unconditional Surrender* (1961).

8. Crick, *Life,* 458–59.

9. Orwell, letter to T. S. Eliot, 28 June 1944, in *Collected Essays,* ed. Orwell and Angus, 3:207.

10. Orwell, letter to Leonard Moore, 18 July 1944, in ibid., 219. Though the book was published later than Orwell had hoped, his wish to remind readers of its precise historical relevance was indicated by his having the period of its composition printed at the end of the text.

11. "As I Please," *Tribune,* 7 July 1944, in ibid., 212.

12. Herbert Read, letter to Orwell, 24 August 1945, quoted in Crick, *Life,* 491.

13. William Empson, letter to Orwell, 24 August 1945, quoted in Crick, *Life,* 492.

14. "Arthur Koestler," in *Collected Essays,* ed. Orwell and Angus, 3:282.

15. 1951, the date of its first appearance in Penguin Books.

16. Cyril Connolly, review of *Animal Farm, Horizon,* September 1945, 215, reprinted in *George Orwell,* ed. Meyers, 199.

17. Orwell mentions *Black Beauty* (but only in passing) in his essay "Riding Down from Bangor," *Tribune,* 22 November 1946.

18. A conflation of two letters: to Julian Symons, 29 October 1948, and to Gwen O'Shaughnessy, 28 November 1948, in *Collected Essays,* ed. Orwell and Angus, 3:510, 518. Orwell also had no love for adders. His brother-in-law, Bill Dunn, described with shocked horror how Orwell on Jura killed a large adder by slitting it open with a penknife. (Crick, *Life,* 525.)

19. Crick, *Life,* 451. Crick notes (453–54) that Orwell had "never previously discussed work in progress with anyone."

20. *Animal Farm* (Harmondsworth, Penguin Books, 1983), 26. Further references follow in the text. See Crick, *Life,* 490: Orwell marked the speech in the copy of *Animal Farm* he gave to Geoffrey Gorer.

21. Snowball's military skill reflects that of Trotsky, who built up the Red Army.

22. The essay was eventually printed as "The Freedom of the Press," *Times Literary Supplement,* 15 September 1972, 1037–39.

23. An example of postwar deterioration of civil liberties that people of Orwell's generation were already well aware of was the retention by the British government after World War I of a measure brought in during it, the Defence of the Realm Act.

24. Crick, *Life,* 449.

25. Graham Greene, review of *Animal Farm, Evening Standard,* 10 August 1945, reprinted in *George Orwell,* ed. Meyers, 196.

Chapter Seven

1. Reprinted in Fredric Warburg, *All Authors Are Equal* (London: Hutchinson, 1973), 103.

2. Crick, *Life,* 563; Anthony Easthope, "Fact and Fantasy in *Nineteen*

Eighty-Four," in *Inside the Myth: Orwell: Views from the Left,* ed. Christopher Norris. (London: Lawrence & Wishart, 1984), 263.

3. *Nineteen Eighty-Four,* ed. Bernard Crick. (Oxford: Clarendon Press, 1984), p. 135. Further references, which follow in the text, are to the *Penguin Complete Novels of George Orwell* (Harmondsworth, England: Penguin, 1983).

4. Printed as Appendix A in Crick, *Life,* 582–84.

5. *Collected Essays,* ed. Orwell and Angus, 3:144.

6. In ibid., 159.

7. *James Burnham and the Managerial Revolution* (London: Socialist Book Centre, 1946). Originally published as "Second Thoughts on James Burnham," *Polemic* 3 (May 1946), reprinted in *Collected Essays,* ed. Orwell and Angus, 4:192–93.

8. Letter to H. J. Willmett, 18 May 1944, in ibid., 3:177.

9. "You and the Atom Bomb," *Tribune,* 19 October 1945, ibid, 4:25.

10. "Toward European Unity," *Partisan Review,* 14, no. 4 (July-August 1947), in *Collected Essays,* ed. Orwell and Angus, 4:424.

11. Review of *We, Tribune,* 4 January 1946, in ibid., 98.

12. E. J. Brown, *"Brave New World," "1984" and "We": An Essay in Anti-Utopia* (Ann Arbor: Ardis, 1976), 45.

13. Letter to Francis A. Henson, 16 June 1949, in *Collected Essays,* ed. Orwell and Angus, 4:564.

14. Brown, *"Brave New World",* 46.

15. Crick, Introduction to *Nineteen Eighty-Four* (Oxford: Clarendon Press, 1984); W. J. West, Introduction to *Orwell: The War Broadcasts* (London: Duckworth/British Broadcasting Corp. 1985).

16. West, Introduction, 64.

17. Letter to Fredric Warburg, 22 October 1948, in *Collected Essays,* ed. Orwell and Angus, 4:507.

18. For the details of this, see Crick, *Life,* 476 ff.

19. Letter to Lydia Jackson ("Elisaveta Fen"), 11 May 1945, in *Collected Essays,* ed. Orwell and Angus, 3:410.

20. In ibid., 28:400.

21. Crick, *Life,* 511.

22. Letter to Michael Meyer, 23 May 1946, in *Collected Essays,* ed. Orwell and Angus, 4:232. Two illustrated articles give an accurate, and attractive, account of Jura and Orwell's connection with it: David Forster, "An Island Remembers," *Scots Magazine,* March 1984, 581–88; Marilyn Green, "Jura: Birthplace of Orwell's *1984,*" *Islands,* April 1984, 78–83.

23. Letter to Leonard Moore, 23 February 1946, in *Collected Essays,* ed. Orwell and Angus, 4:138.

24. Reprinted in Warburg, *All Authors Are Equal,* 103.

25. Crick, Introduction, 118–19. See also 48, for Crick's reservations about the plausibility of Orwell's imaginary society as "a real sociological model."

26. Harold Nicolson, review of *Nineteen Eighty-Four, Observer,* 12 June 1949, 7.

27. Philip Rahv, review of *Nineteen Eighty-Four, Partisan Review* 16, no. 6, (July 1949), 268.

28. A reference (emphasized with bitter parody, 914) to the song "Under the spreading chestnut tree / I loved you and you loved me"; but probably also, as Crick points out, to the Unter den Linden in Berlin, "the street in whose cafés all the conspiracies of Berlin between the wars were supposed to be found" (Crick, Introduction, 449).

29. Trotsky's real name was Bronstein.

30. The notion of this is based on the "Two Minutes' Silence," kept in Britain every 11 November, also at 11:00 A.M., in memory of the dead of both world wars—a typical "Ingsoc" perversion of good into bad.

31. Letter to Leonard Moore, 17 March 1949, in *Collected Essays,* ed. Orwell and Angus, 4:544.

32. The frequency with which Julia addresses Winston as "dear" gives Orwell's presentation of her a strongly individualized flavor. Eileen O'Shaughnessy was thirty when she met Orwell; Julia is twenty-seven when she and Winston meet. Some indirect reference to Eileen's wartime work at the Ministry of Food, and to her interest in food and generosity about it, may be intended in part 2, chap. 4, when Julia brings Winston various "luxury" edibles (i.e. wholesome ordinary foods) only available to the Inner Party. (See Lettice Cooper, "Eileen Blair," in *Orwell Remembered,* 162–66.)

33. There was a St. Cyprian's contemporary of Orwell called E. D. O'Brien, though admittedly he also "loathed" the school. (See Alaric Jacob [another contemporary of Orwell's there], "Sharing Orwell's 'Joys'—But Not His Fears," in *Inside the Myth,* ed. Norris, 72.)

Chapter Eight

1. In *Collected Essays,* ed. Orwell and Angus, 4:579. The title of this chapter is taken from Jacintha Buddicom's poem for Orwell, "Ave Atque Vale," in *The World of George Orwell,* ed. Gross, 7.

2. Malcolm Muggeridge, "A Knight of the Woeful Countenance," in *The World of George Orwell,* ed. Gross, 173.

3. See Crick, *Life,* 579.

4. In *Collected Essays,* ed. Orwell and Angus, 4:573–74.

5. Alex Zwerdling, *Orwell and the Left* (New Haven and London: Yale University Press, 1974), 209.

6. "Lear, Tolstoy and the Fool," in *Penguin Essays,* 410.

7. Reprinted in *Orwell Remembered,* 275.

8. "Reflections on Gandhi," in *Penguin Essays,* 465.

9. Unfortunately, I have been unable to date the issue of *Picture Post* precisely from the single cutting in my possession.

10. Letter to Vernon Richards, 22 June 1949, in *Collected Essays,* ed. Orwell and Angus, 4:566.

11. Reprinted in *Orwell Remembered,* 275.

12. John Atkins, *George Orwell: A Literary Study* (London: Calder & Boyars, 1954), 1: Laurence Brander, *George Orwell* (London: Longmans, Green & Co., 1954), 92, 205.

13. Hollis, *Study of Orwell,* 208.

14. See Daphne Patai, *The Orwell Mystique: A Study in Male Ideology* (Amherst: University of Massachusetts Press, 1984). Also interesting, though far less generally illuminating, are: Beatrix Campbell, "Orwell—Paterfamilias or Big Brother," and Deidre Beddoe, "Hindrances and Help-Meets: Women in the Writings of George Orwell"; both in *Inside the Myth,* ed. Norris.

15. *Orwell: The War Broadcasts,* ed. West, 160.

16. Raymond Williams, *George Orwell* (New York: Viking Press, 1971), 97.

17. "Politics and the English Language," in *Penguin Essays,* 363.

18. Ian Slater, *Orwell: The Road to Airstrip One* (New York and London: W. W. Norton, 1985), 244.

19. "Why I Write," in *Penguin Essays,* 9.

20. George Woodcock, *The Crystal Spirit: A Study of George Orwell* (1966; reprint ed., Harmondsworth, England: Penguin Books, 1970), 81.

21. Zwerdling, *Orwell and the Left,* 150.

22. Woodcock, *Crystal Spirit,* 274.

23. Brander, *George Orwell,* 169.

24. Letter to Tosco Fyvel, 15 April 1949, in *Collected Essays,* ed. Orwell and Angus, 4:559.

25. Crick, *Life,* 571.

26. Letter to Fredric Warburg, 21 December 1948, in *Collected Essays,* ed. Orwell and Angus, 4:519.

27. Quoted in Crick, *Life,* 562.

28. "Why I Write" in *Penguin Essays,* 13.

29. Atkins, *George Orwell,* 269.

30. Woodcock entitled part 3 of *The Crystal Spirit* "The Revolutionary Patriot"; Cyril Connolly, review of *Animal Farm, Horizon,* September 1943, 215.

31. See W. F. Bolton, *The Language of "1984": Orwell's Language and Ours* (Oxford and London: Basil Blackwell & Andre Deutsch, 1984), 46.

32. Atkins, *George Orwell,* 1.

Selected Bibliography

PRIMARY SOURCES

1. Fiction

Burmese Days. New York: Harper & Brothers, 1934. London: Gollancz, 1935.

A Clergyman's Daughter. London: Gollancz, 1935. New York: Harper & Brothers, 1936.

Keep the Aspidistra Flying. London: Gollancz, 1936. New York: Harcourt, Brace & Co., 1956.

Coming Up for Air. London: Gollancz, 1939. New York: Harcourt, Brace & Co., 1950.

Animal Farm. London: Secker & Warburg, 1945. New York: Harcourt, Brace & Co., 1946.

Nineteen Eighty-Four. London: Secker & Warburg, 1949. New York: Harcourt, Brace & Co., 1949.

The Penguin Complete Novels of George Orwell. Harmondsworth, England: Penguin Books, 1983.

Nineteen Eighty-Four. Edited and Introduced by Bernard Crick. Oxford: Clarendon Press, 1984.

2. Nonfiction

Down and Out in Paris and London. London: Gollancz, 1933. New York: Harper & Brothers, 1933.

The Road to Wigan Pier. London: Gollancz, 1937. New York: Harcourt, Brace & World, 1958.

Homage to Catalonia. London: Secker & Warburg, 1938. Boston: Beacon Press, 1952.

The Penguin Complete Longer Non-Fiction of George Orwell. Harmondsworth, England: Penguin Books, 1983.

3. Essays

The Lion and the Unicorn: Socialism and the English Genius. London: Secker & Warburg, 1941.

James Burnham and the Managerial Revolution. London: Socialist Book Center, 1946.

Critical Essays. London: Secker & Warburg, 1946. (As *Dickens, Dali and Others,* New York: Harcourt, Brace & Co., 1946.)

The English People. London: Collins, 1947.

Shooting an Elephant and Other Essays. London: Secker & Warburg, 1950.
England Your England. London: Secker & Warburg, 1953.
Such, Such Were the Joys. New York: Harcourt, Brace & World, 1953.
Collected Essays. London: Secker & Warburg, 1961.
Decline of the English Murder and Other Essays. Harmondsworth, England: Penguin Books. 1965.
The Penguin Essays of George Orwell. Harmondsworth, England: Penguin Books, 1984.

4. Miscellaneous
Introduction to British Pamphleteers. Vol. 1, edited by George Orwell and Reginald Reynolds. London: Allan Wingate, 1948.
The Collected Essays, Journalism and Letters of George Orwell, Edited by Sonia Orwell and Ian Angus. 4 vols. London: Secker & Warburg, 1968. New York: Harcourt, Brace & World, 1968. Reprint. Harmondsworth, England: Penguin Books, 1970.
"The Freedom of the Press." *Times Literary Supplement,* 15 September 1972.
Orwell: The War Broadcasts, Edited by W. J. West. London: Duckworth/British Broadcasting Corporation, 1985.
Nineteen Eighty-Four: The Facsimile of the Extant Manuscript. ed. Peter Davison, London: Secker & Warburg; Weston, Mass.: M&S Press, 1984.

SECONDARY SOURCES

1. Biography and Reminiscences
Buddicom, Jacintha. *Eric and Us: A Remembrance of George Orwell.* London: Leslie Frewin, 1974.
Coppard, Audrey, and Crick, Bernard, eds. *Orwell Remembered,* London: British Broadcasting Corporation, Ariel Books, 1984.
Crick, Bernard. *George Orwell: A Life.* London: Secker & Warburg, 1980. Reprint. Harmondsworth, England, Penguin Books, 1982.
Dunn, Avril. "My Brother, George Orwell." *Twentieth Century,* March 1961, 255–61.
Fyvel, T. R. *George Orwell: A Personal Memoir.* London: Weidenfeld & Nicolson, 1982. Reprint. London: Hutchinson, 1983.
Lewis, Peter. *George Orwell: The Road to "1984".* London: Heinemann/Quixote Press, 1981.
Potts, Paul. "Don Quixote on a Bicycle: In Memoriam George Orwell (1903–1950) for Richard, His Son." In *Dante Called You Beatrice,* 71–87. London: Eyre & Spottiswoode, 1960.
Powell, Anthony. "George Orwell: A Memoir." *Atlantic Monthly,* October 1967, 62–68.

Stansky, Peter, and Abrahams, William. *The Unknown Orwell.* London: Constable, 1972.

——— *Orwell: The Transformation.* London: Constable, 1979.

Symons, Julian. "Orwell, a Reminiscence." *London Magazine,* September 1963, 35–49.

Wadhams, Stephen, ed. *Remembering Orwell.* Markham, Ontario: Penguin Books, 1984.

2. Critical Studies

Apart from a few included in compilations, articles on Orwell are omitted from this list.

Aldritt, Keith. *The Making of George Orwell.* New York: St. Martin's Press, 1961. Traces Orwell's literary development from his rebellion against the symbolist tradition to his creation of the "George Orwell" persona with which to express his response to "social life."

Atkins, John. *George Orwell: A Literary Study.* London: Calder & Boyars, 1954. Sometimes shrewd, sometimes simplistic, this long study, despite its title, is essentially concerned with Orwell's themes and ideas.

Bolton, W. F. *The Language of "1984": Orwell's Language and Ours.* Oxford and London: Basil Blackwell and Andre Deutsch, 1984. Technical study, detailed but very readable, of Orwell's attitudes to, and use of, English, relating these to how the English language has actually developed since his death.

Brander, Laurence. *George Orwell.* London: Longmans, Green & Co., 1954. More literary in its approach than Atkins's book; it is often illuminating, but its simple, declarative style and quasi-official air of approval become irritating.

Calder, Jenni. *Chronicles of Conscience: A Study of George Orwell and Arthur Koestler.* London: Secker & Warburg, 1968. Comparison of Orwell and Koestler as propagandists responding to the political pressures of their age.

Carter, Michael. *George Orwell and the Problem of Authentic Existence.* London and Sydney: Croom Helm, 1985. Presents Orwell's novels as varying attempts to reconcile the individual with society by means of a search for "authentic self."

Gross, Miriam, ed. *The World of George Orwell.* London: Weidenfeld & Nicolson, 1971. Excellently illustrated compendium of essays on various aspects of Orwell's life and work. Particularly stimulating is D. A. N. Jones's "Arguments against Orwell," the devil's advocate's case.

Hammond, J. R. *A George Orwell Companion.* New York: St. Martin's Press, 1982. Sensible, rather than profound, multipurpose book: accounts of Orwell's life and achievement, individual studies, key to "characters and locations," short descriptive bibliography.

Hollis, Christopher. *A Study of George Orwell: The Man and His Works.* London: Hollis & Carter, 1956. Searching, eloquently written, lucid in its exposition of Orwell's narratives, and particularly felicitous in its choice of illustrative quotation.

Hopkinson, Tom. *George Orwell.* Longmans, Green & Co. 1953. Abrasive, irritated, but sometimes admiring pamphlet, marred by numerous small errors of fact.

Hunter, Lynette. *George Orwell: The Search for a Voice.* Milton Keynes: Open University Press, 1984. Sees Orwell's narrative strategies as far more complex and sophisticated than they are generally credited with being, but is itself couched in a dry, abstract terminology that limits its appeal.

Hynes, Samuel, ed. *Twentieth Century Interpretations of "1984".* Englewood Cliffs, N.J.: Prentice-Hall, Inc., 1971. Includes valuable essays by Irving Howe, Stephen Spender, and George Kateb, and an interesting letter to Orwell from Aldous Huxley, who saw the world of *Nineteen Eighty-Four* as leading eventually to that of his own *Brave New World.*

Jensen, Ejner J., ed. *The Future of "Nineteen Eighty-Four".* Ann Arbor: University of Michigan Press, 1984. Contains new essays on *Nineteen Eighty-Four,* including one by Senator Eugene McCarthy, and a penetrating study, "Orwell's Psychopolitics" by Alex Zwerdling.

Kalechofsky, Roberta. *George Orwell.* New York: Frederick Ungar, 1973. Perceptive, crisply written general study of Orwell's work.

Kubal, David L. *Outside the Whale: George Orwell's Art and Politics.* Notre Dame, Ind., and London: University of Notre Dame Press, 1972. Orwell is "one of the paramount figures in modern British literary history," though fully satisfying neither as an artist nor as a political thinker.

Lee, Robert A. *Orwell's Fiction.* Notre Dame, Ind., and London: University of Notre Dame Press, 1969. First study devoted to Orwell as a novelist, and particularly to his management of symbols.

Lief, Ruth Ann. *Homage to Oceania: The Prophetic Vision of George Orwell.* Columbus: Ohio State University Press, 1969. Unduly rhapsodic discussion of Orwell as a defender of basic humanity against political control.

Meyers, Jeffrey. *George Orwell: The Critical Heritage.* London and Boston: Routledge & Kegan Paul, 1975. Brings together over a hundred pieces on Orwell (mostly reviews) from 1933 to 1968.

———. *A Reader's Guide to George Orwell.* London: Thames & Hudson, 1975. Totowa, N.J.: Littlefield, Adams, 1975. Comprehensive and lively commentary.

Meyers, Jeffrey, and Meyers, Valerie. *George Orwell: An Annotated Bibliography of Criticism.* New York: Garland Publishing, 1977. Wide-ranging list of entries, some in other languages than English, with helpful brief comments.

Norris, Christopher, ed. *Inside the Myth: Orwell: Views from the Left.* London:

Lawrence & Wishart, 1984. Generally hostile or "de-mythologizing" essays, concerned to highlight the "right-wing recuperative reading" of Orwell's work and the elements in it that make such a reading possible.

Oxley, B. T. *George Orwell.* London: Evans Brothers, 1967. Sees Orwell as belonging to a tradition of English writers of documentary, and his novels (apart from *Animal Farm,* his single literary success) as being linked through having protagonists who are victims.

Patai, Daphne. *The Orwell Mystique: A Study in Male Ideology.* Amherst: University of Massachusetts Press, 1984. Feminist study of Orwell, taking issue with his limited view of women, and the cult of maleness that underlies his work. Written with clarity and vigor, and often yielding useful insights.

Rees, Richard. *George Orwell: Fugitive from the Camp of Victory.* London: Secker & Warburg, 1961. Valuable view of Orwell's work, admiring but shrewd, by one of his oldest friends, the former literary editor of *Adelphi.*

Sandison, Alan. *The Last Man in Europe: An Essay on George Orwell.* London: Macmillan & Co. 1974. Unusual among Orwell studies in seeing him, despite his agnosticism, as essentially an inheritor of the individualistic Protestant ethic deriving from Luther. *Nineteen Eighty-Four* shows the final defeat of this dissenting intellectual tradition.

Slater, Ian. *Orwell: The Road to Airstrip One.* New York and London: W. W. Norton & Co., 1985. Detailed, rather clotted, study of Orwell's life, work, and ideas, particularly his deepening awareness of the threat of totalitarianism.

Smyer, Richard I. *Primal Dream and Primal Crime: Orwell's Development as a Psychological Novelist.* Columbia and London: University of Missouri Press, 1979. Detailed and cogent examination of the psychological elements in Orwell's writings, and of Orwell's effort "to transform personal attitudes into aesthetically and intellectually satisfying works of art."

Stansky, Peter, ed. *On "Nineteen Eighty-Four".* New York and San Francisco: W. H. Freeman & Co., 1983. Essays on Orwell and *Nineteen Eighty-Four,* by scholars at Stanford University, from a wide range of literary, political, and sociological perspectives.

Steinhoff, William. *George Orwell and the Origins of "1984".* Ann Arbor: University of Michigan Press, 1975. Exceptionally lucid study, focusing on *Nineteen Eighty-Four* as the culmination of Orwell's thinking, and indicating its various literary analogues and predecessors.

Thomas, Edward M. *Orwell.* Edinburgh: Oliver & Boyd, 1965. Sees Orwell's work as full of contradictions, since each book shows him adopting a different persona and relationship to experience.

Voorhees, Richard J. *The Paradox of George Orwell.* West Lafayette, Ind.: Purdue University Studies, 1961. Sees Orwell as a "paradoxical writer": a responsible rebel, a socialist full of reservations about socialism, a man aware of totalitarianism's power but determined to resist it.

Williams, Raymond. *George Orwell.* New York: Viking Press, 1971. Short study that hints, rather than states, a dissatisfaction with Orwell's equivocal socialism: he is part of a historical period, rather than a guide for the future.

———. *George Orwell: A Collection of Critical Essays.* Englewood Cliffs, N.J.: Prentice-Hall, Inc., 1974. Includes particularly valuable essays by Terry Eagleton, Richard Hoggart, Lionel Trilling, John Wain, Stephen J. Greenblatt, and Isaac Deutscher.

Woodcock, George. *The Crystal Spirit: A Study of George Orwell.* Boston: Little, Brown, 1966. Reprint. Harmondsworth, England: Penguin Books, 1970. Comprehensive study, arranged thematically rather than chronologically, of Orwell's personality, ideas, art, and style, bringing acuteness and sympathy to bear on all these areas.

Zwerdling, Alex. *Orwell and the Left.* New Haven and London: Yale University Press, 1974. Though the title genuinely indicates the author's analysis of Orwell's left-wing ideas, this study is equally concerned with Orwell's fictional art, about which it is exceptionally perceptive, seeing Orwell's shortcomings but recognizing their relationship to his concerns as a polemicist.

Index

Adam, Karl, 37
Adelphi, The, 12, 15, 17, 19, 46, 55, 65, 66
Amis, Kingsley, 132
Angel Pavement (J. B. Priestley), 17
Astor, David, 114, 124
Atkins, John, 127, 132, 133
Auden, W. H., 63, 73, 79
Aung, Maung Htin, 11

Ballad of Reading Gaol, The (Oscar Wilde), 12
Baudelaire, Charles, 21
Bevan, Aneurin, 82
Black Beauty (Anna Sewell), 100
Blair, Charles (great-grandfather), 2
Blair, Eileen, nee O'Shaughnessy (wife), 53, 71, 79, 102, 114, 120, 146n32
Blair, Eric. *See* Orwell, George
Blair, Ida Mabel, nee Limouzin (mother), 2, 8, 10, 11, 113
Blair, Marjorie (sister), 2, 64, 114
Blair, Richard Walmesley (father), 2, 8, 10, 113
Blair, Thomas (grandfather), 2, 38
Bolton, W. F. , 132
Bracken, Brendan, 112
Brander, Laurence, 127, 130
Brave New World (Aldous Huxley), 111
Brown, E. J., 111, 112
Buddicom family, 1, 7, 8
Buddicom, Jacintha, 9, 10, 12
Buddicom, Prosper, 8
Burma, 9, 10, 11, 12, 13, 14, 15, 33, 67, 73, 74, 131

Chesterton, G. K., 16, 143n17
College Days, 7
Common, Jack, 54, 67, 76
Connolly, Cyril, 4, 5, 7, 9, 26, 32, 53, 56, 79, 82, 99, 101, 132
Cornford, John, 73
'Country of the Blind, The' (H. G. Wells), 9
Crick, Bernard, 5, 21, 56, 58, 64, 76, 80, 82, 107, 108, 112, 115, 116, 126, 131

Darkness at Noon (Arthur Koestler), 96
Davies, W. H., 20
Death of the Heart, The (Elizabeth Bowen), 117
Dickens, Charles, 9, 17, 41, 89
Dowson, Ernest, 21

Election Times, The, 7
Eliot, T. S., 18, 91, 98
Empson, William, 98, 106
Enemies of Promise (Cyril Connolly), 4, 6
Eton College, 3, 5, 6, 7, 8, 10, 22, 73

Fane, Lady Mary, 2
Faulkner, William, 24
Fields, Dame Gracie, 44
Fierz, Mabel, 17, 18
Fitzgerald, F. Scott, 16
Fontamara (Ignazio Silone), 96
Forster, E. M., 32, 83, 130
Frays College, 34
Frost, Robert, 15
Fyvel, Tosco, 130

Galsworthy, John, 7
Garrett, George ('Matt Lowe'), 66
Gollancz, Victor, 19, 22, 25, 41, 64, 65, 69, 75, 96
Gore, Charles, Bishop of Oxford, 7, 37
Gorer, Geoffrey, 26, 80
Gould, Gerald, 19, 41
Gow, A. S. F., 6, 81, 82
Grapes of Wrath, The (John Steinbeck), 17
Greene, Graham, 107, 125

Greenwood, Walter, 66

Hartley, L. P., 35, 38
'Hawthorns, The' (school), 18, 34
Hayes, 18, 22, 25, 36, 55
Hemingway, Ernest, 16, 56, 79
Henley-on-Thames, 1, 2, 3, 59
Heppenstall, Rayner, 45
Hollis, Christopher, 7, 8, 127, 128, 141n55
Housman, A. E., 14
Huxley, Aldous, 6

Jaques, Eleonor, 25, 33, 36
'Jerusalem' (William Blake), 102
Joyce, James, 16, 40, 132

Katha, 13
Kitchener, Lord, 15
Kopp, Georges, 78

Laski, Harold, 69, 70
Lawrence, D. H., 30, 31, 40, 42, 51, 91
Leavis, F. R., 89
Lee, Robert A., 130
Left Book Society, 69
Limouzin, Nelly (aunt), 13, 16, 44
Longden, Robert, 8
Lord of the Flies (William Golding), 99

Mairet, Philip, 72
Managerial Revolution, The (James Burnham), 109, 110, 118
Maugham, W. Somerset, 29, 32,138n38
Miller, Henry, 24, 26, 27, 35, 57, 94, 95
Mirror of the Past, The (K. Zilliacus), 109
Moore, Leonard, 18, 19, 24
Motihari, 1
Moulmein, 2, 11, 12, 25
Muggeridge, Malcolm, 124
Murry, John Middleton, 17
Myers, L. H., 56
Mynors, Roger, 6

Nicolson, Harold, 116

Orwell, George (Eric Blair): childhood, youth and education, 1–9; death and burial, 124–25; first use of name 'George Orwell', 19–20; in Burma, 10–13; in Jura, 115–16; in Paris, 15–16; in Spain, 72–75; Literary Editor of *Tribune*, 82; meets Eileen O'Shaughnessy, 53; marries Eileen O'Shaughnessy, 71; marries Sonia Brownell, 124; works for B.B.C., 81

WORKS—POETRY:
'Awake Young Men of England,' 5
'Epitaph,' 14
'Kitchener,' 5
'On a Ruined Farm near the His Master's Voice Gramophone Factory,' 55–56, 139n29
'Pagan, The,' 9
'St. Andrew's Day, 1935,' 46

WORKS—PROSE:
Animal Farm, 33, 35, 54, 80, 81, 82, 95, 96–107, 114, 128, 129, 130, 131
'Anti-Semitism in Britain,' 82, 93
'Arthur Koestler,' 96
'Art of Donald McGill, The,' 57, 87–88, 119
'As I Please,' 82, 84, 109
'Benefit of Clergy,' 90–91
'Bookshop Memories,' 46, 86
'Books v. Cigarettes,' 89
'Boys' Weeklies,' 86, 87, 90
Burmese Days, 13, 14, 18, 25–33, 35, 43, 53, 58, 129, 130
'Charles Dickens,' 86, 89
Clergyman's Daughter, A, 17, 18, 34, 35–43, 44, 45, 61, 130, 132
'Clink,' 84
Collected Essays, Journalism and Letters, 82, 84, 124
Coming Up for Air, 3, 26, 34, 37, 39, 54–62, 87, 95, 121, 132, 141n52
Critical Essays, 81, 83
Decline of the English Murder, 83

'Decline of the English Murder,' 87, 88
Down and Out in Paris and London, 1, 15, 16, 17, 19, 20–25, 39, 46, 65, 84
England Your England, 83
'Farthing Newspaper, A,' 16
'Good Word for the Vicar of Bray, A,' 92
'Hanging, A,' 11, 12, 86
Homage to Catalonia, 54, 63, 71–79, 85, 129, 131
'Hop-Picking,' 39, 84
'How the Poor Die,' 15, 86
'In Defence of English Cooking,' 87
Inside the Whale, 81, 83
'Inside the Whale,' 92, 94–95
Keep the Aspidistra Flying, 3, 18, 26, 34, 43–53, 55, 82, 114, 130, 132
'Lear, Tolstoy and the Fool,' 82, 85, 89, 90, 92, 126
Lion and the Unicorn, The, 80–81, 83, 92–93, 94
'Looking Back on the Spanish War,' 76, 85
'Marrakech,' 85
'My Country Right or Left,' 86, 90
Nineteen Eighty-Four, 1, 17–18, 26, 27, 33, 35, 37, 54, 58, 60, 80, 81, 82, 92, 108–23, 124, 126, 128, 130, 131, 132
'Notes on Nationalism,' 82, 93
Penguin Essays of George Orwell, 84
'Politics and the English Language,' 93, 129
'Politics vs. Literature,' 85, 91
'Prevention of Literature, The,' 82, 94, 95
'Raffles and Miss Blandish,' 82, 88
'Rediscovery of Europe, The,' 81
'Reflections on Gandhi,' 85, 126
'Riding Down from Bangor,' 89
Road to Wigan Pier, The, 2, 12, 14, 54, 64–71, 76, 78, 83
Road to Wigan Pier Diary, The,' 64, 65, 66, 69
'Rudyard Kipling,' 90
'Scullion's Diary, A,' 18, 20
'Second Thoughts on James Burnham,' 110
Selected Essays, 84
Shooting an Elephant, 81, 83
'Shooting an Elephant,' 11, 12, 86, 100
'Some Thoughts on the Common Toad,' 92, 117
'Spike, The,' 15, 17, 84, 85, 86
'Such, Such Were the Joys,' 4, 85
'Tolstoy and Shakespeare,' 81
'Toward European Unity,' 110
'W. B. Yeats,' 88
'Why I Write,' 13, 26, 54, 82, 84, 92, 96, 129
'Writers and Leviathan,' 94, 95
'You and the Atom Bomb,' 110

Paris, 13, 15, 18, 20
Passage to India, A, (E. M. Forster), 38
Patai, Daphne, 128
People of the Abyss, The (Jack London), 15
Pitter, Ruth, 15, 17
Plowman, Max, 17
Point Counter Point (Aldous Huxley), 38
P.O.U.M. (Partido Obrero de Unificacion Marxista), 73, 74, 75, 78, 109
Priestley, J. B., 20, 25, 65, 67, 138n39
Pritchett, V. S., 41, 126, 127

Quennell, Peter, 35

Rahv, Philip, 116
Rangoon, 10, 11
Read, Herbert, 98
Rees, Sir Richard, 17, 46
Richards, Vernon, 126
Road to Serfdom, The (F. A. Hayek), 109
Runciman, Steven, 6, 7, 8, 10
Rylands, George, 7

St. Cyprian's School, Eastbourne, 3, 4, 5, 6, 22, 49, 101
Salkeld, Brenda, 35, 40, 45
Sayers, Dorothy L., 140n36
Shakespeare, William, 9, 90
Shaw, George Bernard, 7, 47

Shiplake, 1, 59, 124
Simpson, Louis, 45, 47
Slater, Ian, 129
Southwold, 9, 15, 16, 17, 21, 34, 37, 44
Spender, Stephen, 73, 79
Stonier, G. W., 26
Strachey, John, 69
Sunnylands (school), 2, 3
Sutton Courtenay, 124
Swift, Jonathan, 91, 92, 98, 100, 106
Sykes, Christopher, 25
Symons, Julian, 57, 59

Thomas, Hugh, 75, 79
Turn of the Screw, The (Henry James), 9
Twelfth Night (Shakespeare), 7

van Ghent, Dorothy, 53

Villon, Francois, 60

Wain, John, 132
Wallington, 71, 72, 81, 97, 100, 101
Warburg, Fredric, 108, 113, 115, 131
Waugh, Evelyn, 125
Way of All Flesh, The (Samuel Butler), 7
We (E. I. Zamyatin), 110, 111
Wellington College, 3, 5
Wells, H. G., 7, 57
West, W. J., 112
Wilkes, Vaughan, Mr., 3
Wilkes, Vaughan, Mrs., 3, 4, 5
Williams, Raymond, 129
Willingdon, 101
Winter's Tale, The (Shakespeare), 7
Wodehouse, P. G., 41, 90
Woodcock, George, 129, 132

Zwerdling, Alex, 125, 126, 130